APPLIED MATHEMATICS

Applying Algebra to Everyday Life

Erik Richardson

Cavendish
Square
New York

Published in 2017 by Cavendish Square Publishing, LLC
243 5th Avenue, Suite 136, New York, NY 10016

Library of Congress Cataloging-in-Publication Data

Names: Richardson, Erik.
Title: Applying algebra to everyday life / Erik Richardson.
Description: New York : Cavendish Square Publishing, [2017] | Series: Applied mathematics | Includes bibliographical references and index.
Identifiers: LCCN 2016000624 (print) | LCCN 2016010753 (ebook) | ISBN 9781502619655 (library bound) | ISBN 9781502619662 (ebook)
Subjects: LCSH: Algebra--Popular works.
Classification: LCC QA155 .R54 2017 (print) | LCC QA155 (ebook) | DDC 512.9--dc23
LC record available at http://lccn.loc.gov/2016000624

Editorial Director: David McNamara
Editor: B.J. Best
Copy Editor: Nathan Heidelberger and Rebecca Rohan
Art Director: Jeffrey Talbot
Senior Designer: Amy Greenan
Production Assistant: Karol Szymczuk
Photo Researcher: J8 Media

TABLE OF CONTENTS

Who among us doesn't dream at some point of being the hero—some version of a knight in shining armor?

INTRODUCTION

What is the deal with algebra? When are you ever going to need this out in the real world? I'm not going to lie to you here. What I am going to do is start big and see if I can convince you to agree with me by the end. Ready? Algebra will make your life more awesome. That's it. It can help you be the heroine or the hero that saves the day, defeats the villain, wins the award, discovers the secret, destroys the ring of power, goes back to the quiet, peaceful village at the end and lives happily ever after. You name it.

Here's the thing. We make sense of the world by framing things into stories—whether we realize we're doing it or not. Chances are, if you don't realize you're doing it, maybe that means you are writing a story so unexciting that even you aren't paying attention. Or maybe it means you're coasting and letting other people write your story. If you don't have any goals and don't want any goals, perhaps you won't be interested. I might not be able to convince you that algebra will make your life more awesome. Everyone else? Keep reading.

Whether a story is exciting or dull and dreary depends on which goals the character is pursuing and whether they are making any progress toward them. What if the hobbit wants to save the world, but instead gets lost on his way through the woods and freezes? Not a great story. If he decides not to save the world, but just sits around watching television, again, not a great story. (Hey, hobbits can have TVs in my story if I want them to.)

Still with me? To summarize, big goals, big ideas, and here's the catch. You have to be able to reason backwards from the goal you're after to where you are now. Guess what you need to do that? Algebra. Let's say you need to get to past the dark forest before the winter snows set in. How many miles will you need to cover each day to accomplish that? Will you have enough room left in your pack for the helmet of destiny once you find it? How much other gear can you pack and still have enough room? Will you need your ship to hold together when you go through the wormhole into hyperspace? When will you have to turn on the booster engines to make sure you are going fast enough when you hit the wormhole? To answer these questions, you're going to need algebra.

Heading into this book, that is the one key idea that you should take with you: algebra is about learning how to reason backward so you will be able to achieve whatever goals you're aiming at. When should you push the button on an MRI machine to help detect cancer? How much water pressure to put out the house fire? How long do the people have to evacuate before the **tsunami** hits?

ONE

The History of Algebra

In working to get a better understanding of what is going on in the tangled historical case of algebra, we're going to do the same kind of thing that gets talked about later with regard to analyzing MRI signals. We'll pull some of the key elements apart so we can understand each of them and how they change over time, rather than try to make sense of them while they're all tangled together.

This will take the form of tracing three lines of movement. We'll then look at a contemporary shift that fits into all three of those movements, but cannot be adequately described by them—either individually or taken together. (Please resist the urge to skip to the end of the chapter!)

The March of the Governing Exponents

First, let's look at the simplest of the themes. That is the group of algebra problems that more or less gave shape to each of their successive eras of inquiry.

Here we see Euclid hard at work, trying to fit the world into his geometry.

The earliest stretch of our algebra timeline is anchored in ancient Egypt and Babylon. At that point, mathematicians were almost completely focused on linear and quadratic algebraic equations. As a quick reminder, linear equations take the form of $ax = b$, such that the exponent of the first term (ax) is one. These are called linear equations because in graphing them, the outcomes would all be able to be mapped along a single line. A quadratic equation takes the form $ax^2 + bx = c$. Here we see the leading exponent is a two (x^2).

Tackling these types of equations and working to achieve a general solution to quadratic and cubic equations (with a leading exponent of three) consumed Greek, Hellenic, and Arabic mathematicians until the fifteenth and sixteenth centuries. They could work out specific problems the long way around. But they were looking for a formula that could do for cubic equations what the quadratic formula allowed them to do for any **quadratic equation**.

In the early 1500s, a handful of mathematicians from Italy—del Ferro, Cardano, and Tartablia—each filled in part of the puzzle and allowed, finally, a solution for the generalized cubic equation. They were able to plug in the **coefficients** as had been done with the quadratic formula. It is interesting to note that it was in this process that mathematicians finally came to accept complex numbers and negative numbers, both of which had been points of contention.

It was not long before Ferrari, who had been a pupil of Cardano's, also found a solution to equations of the fourth degree (leading exponent of four). So it will come as no surprise that mathematicians began focusing on finding solutions to quintic equations (leading exponent of five). But in the early 1800's, Niels Abel of Norway and Évariste Galois of France proved that no such generalized solution to fifth-degree equations could exist.

The Form of Expression

In reaching the forms and conventions that we would recognize as algebra, there were really three different stages of development that this branch of math passed through. The first of these is called **rhetorical** algebra. During this phase, equations and formulas were written out in full sentences. Its reign stretched from the ancient Babylonians up to the sixteenth century.

The second major phase is referred to as **syncopated** algebra. Some symbols were used, but they were mixed with a predominantly textual format. This approach made its first appearance in *Arithmetica* by Diophantus around 250 CE. This method had not yet developed some of the symbols that we would now use as exponents, relationships, or operations. It would dominate for the next few centuries.

Then came the phase referred to as symbolic algebra. It was the publication of *La Geometrie* in 1637 by Rene Descartes that

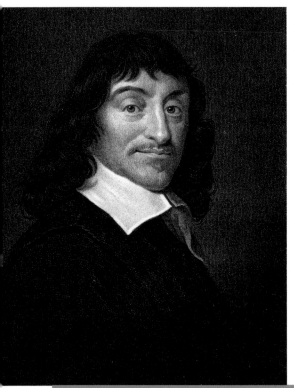

finished the transition to a form we would recognize as algebra today. It might seem puzzling for that to be true of a book that claims to be about geometry. In fact, this work actually reflects the marriage between algebra and the geometric tradition that had faded away after the high point of Greek mathematics.

Rene Descartes was one of the most brilliant minds in history. His way of thinking helped create our modern approach to math and science.

The Father of Algebraic Notation

François Viète (1540–1603) had a successful career in politics and only went into mathematics later in life. When he did, he managed to become one of the most famous French mathematicians of all time.

His text, *Mathematical Laws Applied to Triangles*, was groundbreaking for the way it took a systematic approach, using all six **trigonometric functions**, for doing calculations concerning plane and spherical triangles.

Viète is often called "the father of modern algebraic notation" because he was the first to apply variables to stand in for the unknown parts of an equation. This made it easier to think of the ways that one particular set of numbers fit into an equation, such as how the line equation gives a line for any slope, not just one particular line.

Viète used his practiced talents at **cryptography** (having served for two kings) to break a complex code being used by the Spanish king, Philip II. The king was so certain that his code (and a message five hundred characters long) was unbreakable that when it became clear that the French knew his army's plans, he complained to the Pope, saying that surely some evil sorcery had been done.

Key Cultural Focuses and Impacts

With these three conceptual themes in mind, here is a brief overview of the cultures in which these transformations played out.

Babylonian and Egyptian algebra

As reflected in tablets dated as far back as 1900 BCE, Babylonian algebra had advanced farther than that of Egypt at about the same time. The Babylonian approach appears to focus more on approximate solutions than exact answers. They used linear **interpolation** to narrow possible answers between known values. They also seemed to work with greater interest and depth on quadratic and cubic equations. This is in contrast to the predominant focus on linear equations by the Egyptians, as reflected in the Rhind papyrus from around 1650 BCE in Egypt.

Greek algebra

The next stage of forward development in algebra is centered on Greece and the wider Hellenic region that came under its influence. In Plato's time, the Greeks had developed geometric algebra. Their characteristic approach to solving various algebraic problems was to construct relevant geometric figures and work from those properties or features.

This approach is representative of much of the material in Euclid's *Elements*, the standard text for ages afterward. By way of illustrating this strategy, consider $ax = by$. It is a linear equation that could be thought of as a claim about the area of two rectangles, where a and x are the sides of one rectangle and b and y of another. The Greeks would construct such rectangles, then proceed to show equivalence through the application of geometric principles.

The mathematician Thymaridas lived from about 400 BCE to 350 BCE, and is known for his work with simultaneous linear equations. One of his achievements was a rule, known as the

"Bloom of Thymaridas," which tells us about a relationship between the sum of n quantities and the sum of certain pairs of quantities within that group.

If there is a golden boy of the ancient Greek mathematical world, it is Euclid of Alexandria. He was a Greek living in Egypt under the reign of Ptolemy. Euclid is the grandfather of geometry. His text, *Elements*, an elementary introduction to mathematics, shows not just what certain formulas are, but also sets out a model for how to go about "doing" math. More specifically, it gave a clear blueprint for how to back up claims with proofs that rest on a shared foundation. Because of that, *Elements* became a role model, so to speak, for generalizing a solution past the bounds of specific problems.

Indian algebra

Some of the earliest known evidence of Indian mathematics is a collection of documents dating from around the sixth century BCE. They show engagement with linear and quadratic equations, among other things.

This and other examples of work from the era of Indian preeminence show a broader approach. For example, Indian mathematicians would provide all the integer solutions to a Diophantine equation, whereas Diophantine would only give one. An even larger step forward was demonstrated when an Indian mathematician named Brahmagupta solved the generalized form of the quadratic equation for both the positive and negative roots. He was also an early example of the syncopated form of algebra discussed above.

Islamic algebra

In the flourishing of Islamic mathematics, there seems to be a combination of influences: Babylonian, Hindu, and Greek. While it is important to remember that the Islamic thinkers began the era writing in a purely rhetorical style, they began to transition

This is a sample page from Al-Khwarizmi's algebra text. Notice how there are no diagrams, unlike modern textbooks.

gradually to more syncopated algebra. This can be seen in the thirteenth-century figure of Ibn al-Banna as well as the fifteenth-century figure Abū al-Hasan ibn Alī al-Qalasādī.

The superstar of Islamic mathematical development is Al-Khwarizmi, who died around 850 CE. We actually get the term *algebra* from the title of one of his books on math and astronomy, *Al-jabr wa'l muqabalah*. This famous book carefully walks through the process of solving second-degree **polynomials**. As a key part of its solution process, the text also demonstrates a concept it calls "reduction" and "balancing," referring to things we take for granted. While we see much of the Greek influence in him, this text is also very different in its imitation of Euclid's careful construction style working up from simple building blocks.

A second great Islamic mathematician that deserves mention is the famous poet Omar Khayyam. Not only did his mathematics book on algebra go farther than *Al-jabr*, but his treatment also

A Hit-or-Miss Student

Évariste Galois (1811–1832), was a young mathematician from France who has become legendary for his contributions to the area of **abstract** algebra known as group theory. His primary contribution was a solution to a question that had stumped the brilliant mathematicians of his day. The puzzle was how to figure out when an algebraic equation can be solved by algebraic methods and when it cannot.

Young Monsieur Galois was a hit–or–miss student in spite of his gifted mind, which anyone who has ever had a homework misadventure can relate to. In a story riddled with cosmic unfairness, his great proof showing why quintics (fifth–degree equations) could not be proved algebraically had to be submitted three different times. That means the proof had to be completely rebuilt by hand—there were no photocopiers or hard–drive backups, so he couldn't just make another copy! The first one was misplaced by a professor. The second time he submitted it, the professor he sent it to died, and the paper was lost in the shuffle. The third time, the professors reviewing it couldn't understand the amazing breakthrough he had made in how to attack the problem.

Galois's story comes to a tragic end. The night before he was to die in a duel, he stayed up all night feverishly writing out his ideas and a number of others—also brilliant.

found a way to generalize his solution for all cubic equations with positive roots. At this point in our story, the next major steps forward in algebra take place in Europe.

European algebra

In the period of the Dark Ages, European mathematics reached its low point. Making comments on ancient treatises seemed to be the primary function. However, as the twelfth century was underway, the field saw a virtual explosion of texts that had been translated from the Arabic in a wide range of fields, not just math. By the thirteenth century, Fibonacci's solution of a cubic equation was the real signal of a revival of interest in Europe.

This revival gradually built toward innovations by one of the giants of his time, Gottfried Wilhelm Leibniz. Among his many brilliant ideas is the development of matrix algebra. That's algebra that can be used to work through a number of simultaneous linear equations. (There is a modern example later in the book.) Leibniz recognized that a group of linear equations (called constraints because they each put some limit on possible solutions that would satisfy the whole group of equations) could be arranged in rows and manipulated as whole pieces to help filter the coefficients down to a simplified version. Later work on the idea would result in this process being called Gauss-Jordan elimination.

Leibniz also discovered a **precursor** to Boolean logic, the decision model that would later make computers possible. Further, he developed some versions of symbolic logic that would later prove very relevant to as-yet undiscovered fields of algebra and mathematics.

Abstract Algebra

Finally, here is the strange twist at the leading edge of algebra. It is the sort-of surprise ending mentioned at the beginning of the chapter.

Algebra has gone on to enter a new phase. The vast majority of applied algebra is done the way it has been done for ages, and it continues to be both engaging and highly successful in almost every corner and cabinet on the stage of our shared story. At its leading edge where it grows and explores, it has branched off in a direction that would have been unimaginable in Leibniz's day and age.

It has now turned its attention beyond possible solutions to polynomial equations to a consideration of how whole groups of solutions and types of equations themselves interact and change. Think of it this way: instead of just studying the different kinds of pizzas that are being baked at Papa Piccolo's Pizza Palace, what if we realized we could take the things we had learned from studying pizzas and use them to study the ovens too? What if we wanted to explore the boundaries of what kinds of pizzas are even possible to be made in this kind of oven, not just what kind we made before?

There were plenty of brilliant Islamic and Indian and Greek mathematicians and scientists long before and long after those we have mentioned here. In similar fashion, there was certainly a whole carnival of interesting math things going on during, say, the 1500s, than just trying to find generalized solutions to polynomials of fourth and fifth degrees. The polynomials were just the main act.

But overall, algebra has been a key mathematical process for about three thousand years. The next chapters will consider how it's still at work today.

It's always fun to look out the window of an airport terminal and imagine the interesting places the planes are zooming off to.

TWO

Algebra in Your Everyday Life

With that general overview of the history of algebra in mind, and some sense of how it changed the way we tackle certain kinds of math problems in order to avoid taking the long, slow way around, let's explore some of the ways that it has since settled down into the different areas of our life-o-sphere. (Yes, I made that up just now. It's still a good word—nothing says a newborn word can't be perfectly good.) We need a way to refer to the sort of bubble of experience that moves around with us, complete with the scrolling, background scenery that gives context to whatever storyline we might currently be in and the various possible props and settings we can take up into a given scene.

You should come away with some new perspectives and ideas you can use to develop parts of your own storyline—because you might think about some of it in a new way, but also because you will think about math itself in a new way that makes it a potentially useful tool for you to use.

Vacation

Ah, vacation. Who doesn't like a little down time? Of course, we think, "Hey, let's hop on a plane." For that to happen, though, there is a lot of cool math that has to be in place already and some that has to be calculated along the way. That being said, "Hey, let's hop on a plane!"

Airplanes

For those of you who might take a plane for your trip, you would probably be surprised to learn about the complex type of algebra, called linear algebra, that goes into calculating things like which routes to take, and why some routes are cheaper than others. To really show the math for that, even to explain it, would require a lot of space, so instead let's look at a slightly simpler version of the same idea: how an airline might look at the problem of how many new planes to buy and which kinds.

Let's say an airline is looking to purchase thirty new airplanes, and they know that their goal is to be able to carry 960 new passengers. Pretend that there are only three models of planes to choose from: an eighteen-passenger size, a twenty-four passenger size, and a forty-two passenger size. Take those two requirements and write them like this:

$$x_1 + x_2 + x_3 = 30$$
$$18x_1 + 24x_2 + 42x_3 = 960$$

Keep in mind, the x_1 style just allows us to show they're different kinds of the same thing, not different things. The first line represents the number of planes the airline wishes to buy. The second line represents the different number of passengers each type of plane can hold.

If we write these in a matrix, we can leave off the *x*'s and that will allow us to perform the needed operations without cluttering things up.

$$
\begin{matrix}
1 & 1 & 1 & 30 \\
18 & 24 & 42 & 960
\end{matrix}
$$

Now there are some rules we can apply to try to chop this matrix down so that it fits a certain pattern.

$$
\begin{matrix}
1 & 1 & 1 & 30 \\
18 & 24 & 42 & 960
\end{matrix}
$$

Divide each number in Row 2 by 6.

$$
\begin{matrix}
1 & 1 & 1 & 30 \\
3 & 4 & 7 & 160
\end{matrix}
$$

Then take −3 × Row 1 and add it to Row 2.

$$
\begin{matrix}
1 & 1 & 1 & 30 \\
0 & 1 & 4 & 70
\end{matrix}
$$

Now we need to get a 1 in the middle of Row 1, so we refer to Row 1 as R1 and Row 2 as R2. Then calculate −1(R2) + R1. The process is similar to what we did a step ago.

$$
\begin{matrix}
1 & 0 & -3 & -40 \\
0 & 1 & 4 & 70
\end{matrix}
$$

Now that we have crunched it down to its simplest form, we can put the x's back in and move the pieces around with regular old algebra:

$$1x_1 + 0x_2 + -3x_3 = -40$$
$$0x_1 + 1x_2 + 4x_3 = 70$$

Simplifying these, we get:

$$x_1 - 3x_3 = -40$$
$$x_2 + 4x_3 = 70$$

Two steps happen at this point, and they are both cool. The first is to use a common little trick and pick another letter to substitute into the game at this point to help keep us from getting lost in the different x's. So we will let:

$$t = x_3$$

Now we can rewrite our two equations as:

$$x_1 - 3t = -40$$
$$x_2 + 4t = 70$$

Next, we will move some pieces around:

$$x_1 = 3t - 40$$
$$x_2 = 70 - 4t$$

At this point, we might seem stuck. Solving for two variables in relation to each other without more information looks like something that a) can't be done, or b) at least can't be done without bigger, harder math than we've seen. But wait …

We know that each of these has to be either 0 or bigger than 0. They can't very well buy a negative number of forty-two-passenger jets, for example, can they?

So let's see what happens if we set them equal to 0.

$$x_1 = 3t - 40$$
$$0 = 3t - 40$$
$$3t = 40$$
$$t = 13.3$$

Keep in mind that you can't buy 0.3 jets, so this equation tells us that t must be 14 or higher.

$$x_2 = 70 - 4t$$
$$0 = 70 - 4t$$
$$4t = 70$$
$$t = 17.5$$

This one tells us that to fit within the rules provided (meaning the equations that form the boundaries of the case), 17 is the most t's we could buy.

t	18 passengers	24 passengers	42 passengers
14	2	14	14
15	5	10	15
16	8	6	16
17	11	2	17

So, as long as t (or x_3) is $14 < t < 17$, the mix of jets purchased will work. By plugging each value in for t and cranking the handle around a few times to churn out results, the chart on the previous page gives us a set of possible combinations which will be viable choices for the airline purchase plans.

There are ways to use the same kind of linear algebra to evaluate these different options based on things like price or fuel efficiency, but we'll save that for another time.

One of the things that can make it so challenging for scheduling arrival and departure times (a mystery pondered by almost everyone who has had to race through or wait around in an airport) is that the wind speeds can be a huge factor in either moving planes along or pushing against them and slowing them down in flight.

Consider the following case: Let's say your flight was scheduled to land at 8:00 pm at the end of a 2,400-mile flight. Yet, your captain has just informed you that you are scheduled to land at 8:50 pm. How could that be right? You left plus or minus a few minutes of being on schedule at 1:20 pm. (All these times are based on your watch, not a trick of the time zones.). Well, you're stuck there in the airplane seat, not going anywhere for awhile, so you might as well do a little algebra to while away the time.

We can have:

S = Air speed.
x = Expected speed of flight.
y = Actual speed of flight.

So we know that you left at 1:20 and expected to land at 8:00 for a 2,400-mile trip. That gives us enough information to calculate your base air speed:

$$S_x = 2,400/6:40$$

Converting the minutes part of the time to decimal gives us:

$$S_x = 2,400/6.667 = 360 \text{ mph}$$

In contrast, you are witnessing a flight time of:

$$S_y = 2,400/7{:}30$$

Converting again:

$$S_y = 2,400/7.5 = 320 \text{ mph}$$

Therefore, the impact of wind altering the course of the airplane is:

$$S_x - S_y = 360 - 320 = 40 \text{ mph}$$

You're losing forty miles per hour due to wind blowing into and across the airplane.

Zoo

The Metropolis Zoo has developed plans for a new wolf exhibit that will include a longer travel circuit for the wolves and several new viewing areas for visitors. The project will cost around $15 million, and they have already gotten commitments from major donors totaling $8M of that. With an annual visitor total of 2.5M and a ticket price average of $18 (slightly higher for adults, slightly lower for children under 12), they anticipate a boost of 10% attendance once the new exhibit opens. If they reserve $1.50/ticket from the additional sales toward the expense of developing the new exhibit, and charge an additional $5.50 for the special exhibit ticket for the wolf run and the interactive displays and workshops, how many special tickets does the zoo need to sell each month in order to

A zoo is like a smaller version of the world where we can walk across many continents in just one day.

make up for the cost of the project by the end of ten years?

Let's think about the equation we would need, and then fill in what we've been given in order to see what the missing pieces are. The best place to start is with the equation for breaking even:

To get there, we start from the profit equation:

$$P = \text{Revenue} - \text{Costs}$$

At the moment we break even, there is $0 profit; that's what the term "break even" means.

$$0 = \text{Revenue} - \text{Costs}$$

We just add costs to both sides of previous equation.

$$\text{Costs} = \text{Revenue}$$

Now we need to figure out what the remaining costs are. Remember, of the anticipated $15 million, the zoo already has $8 million accounted for, leaving $7 million to earn over the next ten years.

$$\$7M = \$1.50 \times \text{\# of extra general admission tickets} + \$5.50 \times \text{\# of special exhibit tickets sold}$$

Let's shrink this down to be easier to work with:

x = Number of extra general admission tickets sold
y = Number of special exhibit tickets sold

$$\$7M = \$1.50x + \$5.50y$$

We can figure out how much the zoo expects to make from a boost in general admissions.

$$\text{Increased attendance} = \text{annual average attendance} \times 10\%$$
$$= 2{,}500{,}000 \text{ visitors} \times 0.10$$
$$= 250{,}000 \text{ visitors}$$

$$\text{Additional money raised per year} =$$
$$250{,}000 \text{ additional visitors per year} \times \$1.50$$
$$= \$375{,}000 \text{ per year}$$

$$\text{Total money raised} = \$375,000 \times 10 \text{ years} = \$3,750,000$$

We plug that in:

$$\$7M = \$3,750,000 + \$5.50y$$
$$\$7M - \$3.75M = \$5.50y$$
$$\$3.25M = \$5.50y$$

This allows us to solve to find out what y needs to be:

$$\$3,250,000 \,/\, \$5.50 = \text{number of tickets that have to be sold to break even} = 590,909.09 \text{ tickets}$$

That's a ten-year total, so if they sold the same amount from one year to the next, they would need to sell 59,090.90 (59,091 tickets) each year. The director drills down a little to see if there are particular patterns to the attendance numbers each year, and he notices that, in fact, the year is not smooth. Rather, it is much higher over the summer months. In fact, almost 60% of their annual visitor totals happen during the months of June, July, and August. How would this impact the forecast? At the end of June, how would they know if they were on track to hit their target?

$$59,091 \text{ tickets} \times 60\% = \text{summer sales}$$
$$= 35,454.60, \text{ which rounds up to } 35,455 \text{ tickets}$$

So, they need to sell 35,455 tickets in June. Does that make sense? No! Don't give in so easily. In June, they only need to hit 1/3 of that summer goal, which is 11,818.33. Rounding tells us that if they hit 11,818 tickets, they are pretty much on track.

Zoos also let us walk back in time. Wolves were one of the first animals humans domesticated tens of thousands of years ago.

Zoos in America

There are more than ten thousand zoos and aquariums around the world, with 230 of those being in the United States. Each year in America, there are over 180 million visitors—more than attendance at NBA, NFL, NHL, and MLB events all put together.

In looking at a fairly typical zoo in a big city, in just one month a zoo can go through more than 45,000 pounds (20,412 kilograms) of hay, 14,000 pounds (6,350 kg) of fruit and veggies, and 15,000 pounds (6,804 kg) of fish and meat. One zoo even included some of the items on their annual shopping list; it can save money to buy the food and store it at the zoo. Among the things listed were: 20,000 pounds (9,072 kg) of carrots, 15,000 pounds (6,804 kg) of bananas and—weirdly enough—75 pounds (34 kg) of earthworms (don't ask!).

While we often think of the money we pay into the zoo, we don't always realize the money that flows from the zoo out into the surrounding community. Zoos contribute almost $16 billion to the US economy each year—not only in terms of jobs created but also in terms of their spending on new or updated exhibits and maintenance projects. Beyond the direct impact on the economy, studies have shown that visitors have a stronger awareness of the importance of various conservation efforts, which makes a long-term, indirect impact on the community.

Restaurants

A restaurant can be a festival of sights and tastes and smells. But just under the surface, it is also a veritable carnival of numbers and equations.

Consider, for example, that every price on the menu is the result of a careful mathematical process between supply and demand functions. Imagine that Brendan, the owner of a bakery called the Crusty Baker, recently came up with a new kind of pie and has been testing out different prices to see how it sells before adding it to his permanent menu. After collecting information on it for a couple of weeks, he plugs the data into a program that does a little crunching and coughs out a formula to represent what his measurements show. The formula is:

$$y = -0.25x^2 + 8.5x - 24$$

The below graph shows this equation.

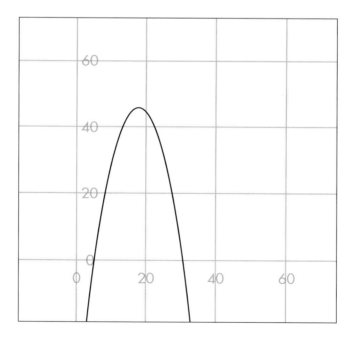

A baker looking at a tray of rolls doesn't just see rolls. He also sees temperature and volume, as well as connected curves on a graph.

What Brendan wants to figure out from this is: at what production level will he sell the most pies? He could estimate from looking at the graph, but going over or under could have a big impact on sales as well as wasted ingredients and work time. To pin it down more carefully, Brendan works the following formula to find the **midpoint** of the curve (in downward facing curves like this, the midpoint is the highest point):

$$y = -b/2a$$

Remember, the profit formula up above is in the form $y = ax^2 + bx + c$, so we know:

$$a = -0.25$$
$$b = 8.5$$

Plugging those values in gives us:

$$y = -8.5/(2 \times -0.25)$$
$$y = 17$$

So to make the **maximum** profit, Brendan should aim to make seventeen of the new pies each week.

A closely related question: What is the **minimum** number of the new pies he should make each week to avoid losing money? Notice on the graph above that the minimum is the place to the left of the high point where the profitability curve hits zero before sinking into the loss category.

Places where a function, like a **parabola**, hit the x-axis have a $y = 0$. In order to find the places where the profit is zero, we need to break the function open. In Brendan's case, he just punches the numbers into his computer to get it to do the process, but the trade-off is that he is not using it in his own head, so the understanding of why it works or what it's doing under the surface can fade away.

Instead, imagine he uses a quadratic equation:

$$\frac{-b \pm \sqrt{(b^2 - 4ac)}}{2a}$$

Now, we just need to plug Brendan's numbers into the equation and crank the handle until answers come out.

$$y = -0.25x^2 + 8.5x - 24$$

$$= \frac{-8.5 \pm \sqrt{(8.5^2 - 4 \times -0.25 \times -24)}}{(2 \times -0.25)}$$

$$= \frac{-8.5 \pm \sqrt{(72.25 - 24)}}{(-0.5)}$$

$$= (-8.25 \pm 6.95)/(-0.5)$$

We need to break the "plus or minus" into its separate parts:

$$y = (-8.25 + 6.95)/-0.5 = 2.6$$
$$y = (-8.25 - 6.95)/-0.5 = 30.4$$

So if he makes less than 2.6 or more than 30.4 pies, he will lose money. Obviously he's not looking to make 0.6 pies, nor 0.4 pies, so in order for him to still make money, we can set the boundaries at 3 and 31.

A second, common problem that comes up in the constant process of providing customers with new items to try is the attempt to create some new products with a **predictable** cost level, so you are able to hit a close estimate for pricing on your first attempt.

Consider the situation at the fictional Caffeine Carnival Gourmet Coffee Shop. Owner Colleen wants to put together a new blend to sell. She wants to mix Sumatra coffee, which costs $2.50 per pound, with Colombian coffee that costs $3.75 per pound. She plans on making fifty pounds of mix with the cost of the mix coming out to $3.35 per pound. How many pound of each type of coffee will she need?

Pounds of Sumatra (s) + pounds of Colombian (c) = 50:

$$s + c = 50$$

Price of Sumatra × pounds of Sumatra + price of Colombian × pounds of Colombian = price of mixture × total pounds:

$$\$2.50s + \$3.75c = \$3.35 \times 50$$

Take the first equation and solve for either letter—in this example, s.

$$c = 50 - s$$

Substitute 50-s in for c in the first equation:

$$2.50s + 3.75(50 - s) = 167.50$$

Distribute the 3.75:

$$2.50s + 187.50 - 3.75s = 167.50$$

Combine like terms:

$$187.50 - 1.25s = 167.50$$

Subtract 187.50 from both sides:

$$-1.25s = -20$$

Divide by 1.25:

$$s = 16$$

So Colleen needs sixteen pounds of Colombian coffee, leaving thirty-four pounds of Sumatra coffee to add up to fifty.

Finding equilibrium price

One of the interesting things to realize is that every price you see on the menu at the coffee shop or the bakery is the result of a kind of tug-of-war between two different linear equations. One is an equation that represents the demand for a product at different prices. The other is an equation that represents the willingness of the business to make and sell more of the item at each different price, known as supply.

Solving the problem in this case works the same way you see elsewhere, but there are two things worth noting: one is that the more you learn about math, the more you see that things in very different situations share certain similarities that allow us to apply a math strategy or model from one area to another one. (That's huge! That makes us smarter and saves us tons of time.) The second is to see that even though the "shape" of the math is the same, the impact on something back in the real world can be very different. How long to spend on the first part of a canoe trip or which cell phone plan is the best are very different decisions than, "Should I buy this pecan pie?"

Let's see an example of how these two linear equations duke it out to settle on a price where both of them are mostly happy. Suppose our baker, Brendan, is trying to figure out the right price to charge when people only want to buy half of a pie. He needs to be careful, because the chance of matching up exactly the right number of people who want half of the same pie during a day is too low, and some halves of pies will get wasted.

Let's have the equation representing customer demand be:

$$p = -0.3q + 5$$

Meet John Cerny

We sat down with John Cerny from Great Harvest Bread Company.

Thanks for taking your hands out of the bread dough to talk with us, John. How long have you been with Great Harvest?

I've been an owner for five years now.

I've mentioned to people how math can sometimes feel like pair of clip-on sunglasses that sort of add a layer that we look at the world through. Does it seem like that to you sometimes?

Oh, sure. In order to find out my daily bake forecast, I'm always averaging the previous two weeks' numbers and checking for trends, and so on. I also spend a lot of time thinking about things in terms of fractions. For example, if I need fifteen loaves of nine-grain bread, that is a quarter batch; thirty is a half batch, etc. However, if I need twenty-two loaves, then we call it a "quarter plus" or "quarter and an eighth." Then once stuff is in the rising ovens, we are constantly checking the temps. If a dough is too hot, it could proof too fast and "die," whereas if it's too cold, it may not get big enough.

Temperature regulation must be challenging with ovens cycling up and down throughout the day.

It's tricky. The temperature of the bakery is always a factor. In the summer heat, bread proofs faster. In the cold of winter, bowls are cold so the dough needs more time to rise.

What are some of the ways you feel like math has the biggest impact?

I'm always gauging sales versus labor, so I have to factor in sales and payroll versus cost of goods, and so on. When you look at things around you or stuff happening, you're seeing it from two different points of view, you know?

Is there a kind of math problem or application that seems kind of cool or different compared to "regular old stuff you did in school?"

I'm always using numbers with the bread forecast and averaging. I'm also always watching when employees interact with the customers. I'm thinking about if the customer seems happy, and at the same time I'm looking at what is on the counter, quickly estimating what the total should be and then noticing that they may be over or under by too much.

Interesting! Thanks for sharing your perspective with us.

And the equation for supply be:

$$p = 0.06q + 0.68$$

where:

q = Quantity of halves of pies.
p = Price in dollars.

Think about what the demand equation is saying. If the price were just \$0.50, then customers would be willing to buy:

$\$0.50 = -0.3q + 5$, which comes out to 15 half pies per day

But they would be willing to buy only 5 if the price were:

$$p = -0.3 \times 5 + 5 = \$3.50$$

In contrast, if the price were \$3.50, the supplier would only be interested in selling:

$\$3.50 = 0.06q + 0.68$, which comes out to 47 half pies per day

But he would only be willing to sell 5 of them if the price were:

$$p = 0.06 \times 5 + 0.68 = \$0.98$$

See how they are kind of pulling in opposite directions?

So, we need to set the two equations equal to each other. If they were graphed, the two lines would intersect at that point:

$$-0.3q + 5 = 0.06q + 0.68$$

Subtract 0.68 from both sides:

$$-0.3q + 4.32 = 0.06q + 0$$

Now add $0.3q$ to both:

$$0 + 4.32 = 0.36q$$

Here's the part where we see the homestretch. Divide everything by 0.36:

$$12 = q$$

That's the quantity where the two meet up. Then we plug that back in to find p:

$$p = -0.3 \times 12 + 5 = \$1.40$$

So, Brendan should set the price to $1.40, the **equilibrium** price. He can expect customers will buy 12 halves of pies. At this price, he will make the most money with the fewest wasted resources.

The Great Outdoors

I'm on a boat

For some people, sailing is the perfect example of breaking free and escaping, away from land and noise. For others, sailing means racing with the same adrenaline and competitiveness that the others were trying to escape. In either case, there are patterns and formulas that govern how the wind and waves and sails interact. Let's take a look at one of those formulas.

Algebra allowed us to master wind and waves breaking out past the sight of our home shores.

The formula for sail area-**displacement** (S) gives a good measurement for how much power a sail can have. Let's look at an example:

A = Sail area in square feet.
d = Pounds of displacement. This is the weight of the water the boat pushes away by being in the water.

Here is the formula:

$$S = 16Ad^{-2/3}$$

So if we have a ship with a sail area of 808 square feet and displacement at 24,234 pounds, we can solve for S:

$$S = 16 \times 808 \times 24{,}234^{-2/3} = 15.438 \text{ lbs}$$

This final number is applied to a scale. This particular sail power is good for large boats that can sail across oceans.

Hiking/camping

In the case of something like packing for a backpacking trek, even when we have mathematical tools ready, we still need to do some math to make the tool apply to this particular situation. In figuring out the best route, experienced hikers understand the effect that backpacks of different weights can have on their pace, which, in turn, affects their plans on locations for overnight camping sites along the way. It can also affect their need for **supplemental** equipment, like wraps or soft braces.

Below we have a reference chart that shows what an experienced backpacker has learned about his pack weight

Number of days	0.5d + 30 =	2.5d + 30 =
1	30.5	32.5
2	31	35
3	31.5	37.5
4	32	40
5	32.5	42.5

Meet Will Marquardt

This is Will Marquardt, a seasoned pro at outdoor adventure and the owner of Outdoors Geek, a rental shop for all kinds of outdoor recreation gear.

Great that you could share your insights with us, Will. Can you share some perspective on what math has to do with your work?

You're talking to the right guy. Math is part of every single facet of what we do—from keeping track of inventory and **thermal** ratings on a warehouse of gear we rent out, to taking people who are new to camping and hiking and helping them walk through some of the math involved in a successful wilderness outing. Very often the only math they see is a price tag, but that's not telling them as much as they imagine. They need the rest of the numbers to help make better choices.

Cool. Can you give us a few examples of those underlying numbers you try to get them to think about?

Here are a couple of great examples. Even after you walk them through one, they turn around and do it again on a different issue, and that's volume versus weight. At the same time, I have to walk newbies through this, because there are those people who try to pack five hoodies. I explain about thermal ratings and lightness and how quickly stuff will dry, and they're like, "Got it!" Then they turn around and start making the same mistake about their food. They'll load stuff in that is bulky and "seems like a good idea," but doesn't have high calories or high protein that you need on a trip when the car might be miles away.

What's the biggest mistake you think people make?

Hard to pick, but I know my top two. Not knowing how to navigate with a map and compass. Even if they have GPS, sometimes they don't understand enough about latitude and longitude to actually find their way out in a crisis.

And the second?

Trying to ignore the numbers. How do you pick a good sleeping bag without comparing apples to apples by looking at the numbers *and* by understanding how they come up with those numbers? The same is true for packs, boots, and everything else you might need.

So, do you guys rent out hoodies? Just kidding! Thank you for talking with us, Will.

Pack Weight Based on Temperature

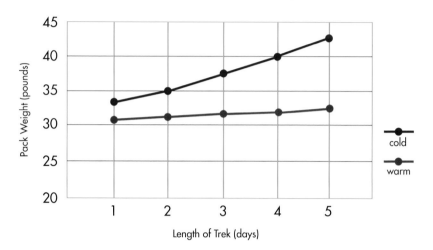

relative to the expected weather. He has found that for a mid-summer hike lasting d days, in weather averaging 80°F—which means less food and lighter/fewer clothes are needed—can be represented by the formula:

$$W = 0.5d + 30$$

where his frame pack weighs 30 pounds.

In contrast, the formula for his packed pack weight during a cold-weather hike with temperatures averaging closer to 40°F is:

$$W = 2.5d + 30$$

There's a great opportunity for him to join a group hiking part of the Appalachian Trail next month, and the weather for the five-day stretch that he can join them is forecast to hover in the range between 55 and 60 degrees. What good is his chart now?

Surprise! There might be some *doing of math* to figure out his pack weight. Now, since the "+ 30" part would stay the same, the only thing we really need to puzzle about is what the appropriate coefficient for *d* would be. That would tell us what to use as the slope for a line that runs in between.

We can see what we're up against if we put together a quick table:

The formula for interpolation (finding a missing point in a graph) is:

Average Temperature (°F)	Coefficient (slope)
40	2.5
57.5	?
80	0.5

$$y(x) = y_1 + \frac{x - x_1}{x_2 - x_1}(y_2 - y_1)$$

So we can take the two measures given (40, 2.5) and (80, 0.5) and plug them into the equation.

$$y(x) = 2.5 + \frac{57.5 - 40}{80 - 40}(0.5 - 2.5)$$

$$y(x) = 2.5 + [(17.5/40) \times -2.0]$$

$$y(x) = 2.5 + 0.4375 \times -2.0$$

$$y(x) = 1.625$$

The Appalachian Trail

The Appalachian Trail stretches from Georgia to Maine—fourteen states and 2,185 miles along the Appalachian Mountains. Started in 1921 by private citizens, it took sixteen years to finish and opened in 1937. Several groups share responsibility for the trail today, including the Appalachian Trail Conservancy, the National Park Service, and the US Forestry Service, along with help from thousands of volunteers.

In reading about the Trail, it is common to find the claim that it takes five million steps to get all the way from one end to the other, and most estimates say that it takes an average hiker between five and seven months to hike the entire trail.

This brings up an interesting and entertaining fact about numbers like this, though: that average is only based on people who complete it. If we divided the average to include everyone who started out with the goal of completing it, we would have a much higher number as our average.

From the backpack case a few minutes ago, you will have some appreciation for how hard it is to pack well *and efficiently* for the Appalachian Trail, because of the time it takes to travel stretches over a range of seasonal changes, but on top of that are the big swings in conditions as you go up or down in **altitude** on a given day.

Let's do a quick check. Does this new slope seem reasonable? Well, we know from the table above that the slope is somewhere between 0.5 and 2.5. Our interpolated slope of 1.625 makes sense, as it fits between those numbers.

That knowledge allows us to find the new equation we would use to calculate the expected weight. The new equation is:

$$w = 1.625d + 30$$

For those of you who might have thought, "Hey, let's just drop some cross-multiplication on this thing," that would have caused mistakes. To quickly prove that, let's compare the results we would have gotten:

In case 1:

$$2.5/80 = x/57.5$$
$$(2.5 \times 57.5)/80 = 1.797$$

In case 2:

$$0.5/40 = x/57.5$$
$$(0.5 \times 57.5)/40 = 0.719$$

So, as you can see, that's not always the best way to attack a problem. In this case it seems to make only a small difference, but sometimes a small difference in the math could mean a big difference to your health or happiness. Think how much faster it is to fix the math than, say, sit around waiting for the medical response team because your ankle gave out because you didn't think you'd need ankle supports. Right?

But, hey, you didn't. You were smart, and you walked through the math the right way. We saw that in warm weather the five-day trip would give a result of 32.5 pounds for the backpack, while the cold weather trip would give a result of 42.5. What would we get in the new case? If we're lucky, it should fall in between:

$$w = 1.625 \times 5 + 30$$
$$w = 8.125 + 30$$
$$w = 38.125 \text{ lbs}$$

It makes sense. Great!

Canoe trek

Maybe sailing isn't your thing. Maybe you're more the canoeing type. Let's see an example of how algebra would be a handy tool to pack in a waterproof bag with the rest of your gear.

You rent out the canoes for eight hours, and on your trip, you need to figure out what time to turn back so you don't get charged extra for overnight rental after the office closes. Now you know that your normal lake pace with no wind is right around 5.5 mph. On your way upstream, you track against the first few mile markers and see that you're making about 4 mph. The question is: how does math step in here and help you get the most out of your canoe trip?

Use this formula:

x = Hours traveling upstream.
y = Hours traveling back downstream.

Now think about the different rates. We know your upstream rate is 4 mph. Does that give us enough information to figure out what the downstream rate will be? Well, with your upstream rate and your calm-lake rate, we can figure out how fast the river's current is running.

$$5.5 \text{ mph} - c = 4 \text{ mph}$$

Pretty easy, right? The river is pulling at 1.5 mph. So the rate coming back downstream will be:

$$5.5 \text{ mph} + 1.5 \text{ mph} = 7 \text{ mph}$$

If we have two usable equations, it will be game on.

$$x + y = 8 \text{ hours}$$

And we know you need to travel as far back as you travelled out.

$$4x = 7y$$

Sweet! Let's get one of the variables alone in the first equation and then use substitution into the second equation to solve for the other one.

$$x = 8 - y$$
$$4(8 - y) = 7y$$
$$32 - 4y = 7y$$

Now we add $4y$ to both sides:

$$32 = 11y$$

Divide everybody by 11:

$$2.9091 \text{ hours} = y$$

Then we can plug that back into our first equation to find x:

$$x + y = 8$$
$$x + 2.9091 = 8$$

$$x = 5.091 \text{ hours}$$

So, we have about five hours of paddling upstream, and three hours to return. But to be exact, the next step is up to you. You can do the **conversion** to see how many minutes 0.091 of an hour equals for traveling upstream, and how many 0.9091 equals for returning. Or you could round, because decimals aren't easy to calculate in your head. You could round to 5 and 1/10th of an hour, which become five hours and six minutes (1/10th of an hour = 6 minutes). Then the return trip would be two hours and fifty-four minutes. Let me leave you with a question to consider: how would you adjust the equation if you wanted to have an hour at your farthest point to beach the canoe and have a small campfire lunch?

Snowboarding

If we managed not to get eaten by wild bears on the camping trip, and we managed not to drown or go over the falls on the canoe trip, that must mean it's time to see how many bones in the ankle can be broken by hurtling down the snowboarding hill at Mach 1. Actually, on second thought, let's send Brendan and Colleen. They've both needed a reason to get away from the bakery and the coffee shop, so this will be perfect, and, if anyone gets hurt, remember, they're fictional.

So Brendan and Colleen made it over to the Alpine Adventures ski park to do some snowboarding. They stuck with the amateur hill, which only climbs at an angle of 30°, but it felt dangerous enough to make them happy. It took them a couple tries to get all the way down the hill without falling or stalling out. On their third time down, they decided to time themselves to see how fast they were going. Colleen made to the end line in 190 seconds, and Brendan was close behind at 194 seconds.

The run is 2,000 feet, according to the trail map. But if the map hadn't included this information, they could have figured it out because the incline angle and the height of the hill would have allowed them to determine it from the special property of 30-60-90 triangles. So:

$$R = d/t$$

R_b = Brendan's rate of speed.
t_b = Time for Brendan to complete the run.
R_c = Colleen's rate of speed.
t_c = Time for Colleen to complete the run.
d = Distance.

So for Colleen:

$$R_c = d/t_c$$
$$R_c = 2,000 \text{ ft}/190 \text{ s}$$
$$R_c = 10.53 \text{ ft/s}$$

Then for Brendan:

$$R_b = d/t_b$$
$$R_b = 2,000 \text{ ft}/194 \text{ s}$$
$$R_b = 10.31 \text{ ft/s}$$

Now let's create the conversion factor to get miles per hour:

$$= \frac{1 \text{ mi}}{5,280 \text{ ft}} \times \frac{60 \text{ sec}}{1 \text{ min}} \times \frac{60 \text{ min}}{1 \text{ hr}}$$

$$= 3,600 / 5,280$$
$$= 0.68182 \text{ mi/hr}$$

$$R_c = 10.53 \times 0.68182 = 7.18 \text{ mph}$$
$$R_b = 10.31 \times 0.68182 = 7.03 \text{ mph}$$

Triathlons

Some people don't want to have to make a choice about which kind of nature outing to go on, so with ambition and perseverance, they attempt—in a way—to take in all of nature in one shot by participating in triathlons. A triathlon is a long-distance race that has three phases, usually swimming, bicycling, and running.

Let's look at some of the different ways that algebra could play a role in real-life situations for a triathlete in the course of her training and in competition. Imagine that there is a competitor named Amelia, it's race day, and that she is looking to finally break the 3-hour mark this year. Here is the format of the race:

Swim 1 mile
Bike 25 miles
Run 5 miles

She's been training at paces a little faster than the 3-hour boundary because she knows the actual adrenaline in her system on race day adds some fatigue over the course of the triathlon. She has calculated out the paces she needs to hit at the race, and they are:

Swim 1 mile: Her training pace is 2 mph:

$$2 \text{ mi}/1\text{hr} = 1\text{mi}/x$$

Cross-multiply and divide:

$$x = (1 \times 1)/2 = 1/2 \text{ hr} = 30 \text{ minutes}$$

Bike 25 miles: Her last pace was an average of 15 mph:

$$15 \text{ mi/1 hr} = 25 \text{ mi/}y$$

Cross-multiply and divide:

$$y = (25 \times 1)/15 = 1.667 \text{ hr} = 1\tfrac{2}{3} \text{ hr} = 1 \text{ hour,}$$
$$40 \text{ minutes}$$

Run: Her recent training pace average is 6 mph:

$$6 \text{ mi/1 hr} = 5 \text{ mi/}z$$

You'll never guess what happens now…cross multiply and divide!

$$z = (5 \times 1)/6 = 5/6 \text{ hr} = 50 \text{ minutes}$$

That puts her exactly at the three-hour mark when she hits the finish line. Knowing she won't be able to do some of this in her head on race day, and since she knows the bike is her weakest event, but running her strongest, she goes ahead and calculates out what she would have to do if she is behind her pace coming into the last part of the event. If she is down by 1 minute, she needs to move her pace up by:

$$60 \text{ sec/5 miles} = 12 \text{ sec/mile}$$

So now instead of 10min/mile, she needs to run 9:48 per mile. We'll convert minutes to a decimal, so we can do the math.

$$t = 48/60$$
$$t = 0.8 \text{ minutes}$$

We add 0.8 to the 9 minutes, and calculate the **proportion**:

$$9.8\text{min}/1\text{mile} = 60\text{min}/n_1 \text{ miles}$$

where n_1 is the new mph she would need.

$$6.12245 \text{ mph} = n_1$$

To understand what that really means, we need to think of it as a percent improvement over her previous best run time.

$$C_p = (\text{New value} - \text{Beginning Value})/\text{Beginning Value}$$
$$C_p = (6.12245 - 6.0)/6.0 = .02 = 2\%$$

With this picture in mind, Amelia decides to train to reach that faster pace. She'll begin five weeks out from the triathlon, and then slow down her training leading into the race. Her plan is that each week she will cut 10% off the pace of her weekly run time. In the last week, what percentage of her original pace will she be at?

Now we could do it the long way and run out five calculations, but, hey, we have mad math powers, right? And math powers mean shortcuts! We can use a version of the same formula that calculates interest in your bank account. That one is:

$$A = (1 + r/n)^{nt}$$

where:

r = The interest rate each year.
n = The number of periods during the year interest is calculated.
t = The number of years over which the interest is being accumulated.

In Amelia's case, though, the percent is being taken out, so we will have a minus in the middle. Since it is only happening one time each week for 5 weeks, we can remove the *n* in our version.

$$A = (1 - .10)^5$$

So that would give us a result of:

$$A = 0.59049 = 59\%$$

This means her training pace on the final week before the race will be her new, faster rate adjusted down to 59%. Her training pace would be 6.12 mph × 59% = 3.61 mph.

Reducing her training pace helps prevent injuries from running too hard right before the triathlon. By reducing by 10% each week, the drop is staying proportional—otherwise, her body would feel like it was getting a bigger and bigger drop each time, and it might not respond to training as well as she needs it to.

Safety in the Air, on Land, and Sea

There are two particularly well-hidden ways that mathematical equations are part of the ropes and pulleys that keep the world around us safe and running relatively smoothly. The first is the blanket of security created by our armed forces. The second is about the electronic web that has been laid over us by our Internet and cell phones. Perhaps by now you are noticing some math at work in ways that seem invisible to us in our day-to-day lives. That's a little cool, don't you think?

Consider this military example. An aircraft carrier and its accompanying strike group left port traveling west at about 25 mph. Three hours later, one of the nuclear submarines in the strike group finished repairs and left port to catch up with the group. The sub established cruising speed of 30 mph to overtake them. How can the group figure out the time to rendezvous?

Twenty-five miles per hour (40 kmh) might not seem fast, but for a small city with about six thousand people, more than sixty planes, and all necessary supplies, that is crazy fast.

The basic formulas relate time and **velocity** (which is speed as a rate, such as miles per hour) with distance travelled:

$$\text{Distance} = \text{velocity} \times \text{time, or } d = vt$$

Since they are travelling at different rates, we will need a separate equation for each of them. For the carrier, that would be:

$$d = 25 \text{ mph} \times t \text{ hours}$$

In the case of the submarine, keep in mind that it left 3 hours later, so however long the carrier has been travelling (t), the sub has been travelling 3 fewer hours (t-3). So the equation for the sub is:

$$d = 30 \text{ mph} \times (t - 3) \text{ hours}$$

At the point these two meet, the equations have to equal the same number. So we put them together:

$$25 \text{ mph} \times t \text{ hours} = 30 \text{ mph} \times (t - 3) \text{ hours}$$
$$25t = 30t - 90$$
$$-5t = -90$$
$$t = 18 \text{ hours}$$

If I had a dollar for every time I've been tripped up by a simple calculation error, I'd be writing this book from a remote island somewhere. So, let's check to make sure. If the aircraft carrier and the rest of its strike group travelled for 18 hours, that would be:

$$25 \times 18 = 450 \text{ miles}$$

For the sub, it travelled:

$$30 \times (18 - 3), \text{ so } 30 \times 15 = 450 \text{ miles}$$

Boom! Perfect.

Interceptor

In another scenario, a base registers an aircraft crossing a no-fly zone and approaching the base's defensive outer **perimeter** at speed of 730 miles per hour (just below Mach 1, the speed of sound). It is 158.2 miles and closing on the first perimeter. Analysis suggests it is an unmanned drone, so the colonel orders two F/A-18 fighters to prep for launch and hold at standby.

Drones like this one weigh and cost only a fraction of what a manned aircraft costs.

At the current drone speed, the time it would take to fly between the outer perimeter and the inner perimeter (where the colonel orders the F/A-18s to engage) is 4.1 minutes, and in 20.1 minutes, it could reach the air base.

The fighter jets can go 1,190 mph (almost Mach 2). How long before the fighter planes would need to launch to **intercept** at the outer perimeter? But the air base doesn't want to scramble jets if this is only an attempt to increase tensions, so the colonel also wants to know: How much time is there before she has to launch the fighters to fire on the drone at the moment it breaches the inner perimeter, which is 200 miles away?

If they want to allow the jets to meet the drone at the outer perimeter, we first need to know when the drone will reach it.

$$730 \text{ miles/hour} = 158.2 \text{ miles/}x$$

For simplicity, we'll convert to minutes.

$$730 \text{ miles} / 60 \text{ min} = 158.2 \text{ miles/}x$$

Cross multiplying gives us:

$$(158.2 \times 60)/730 = 13$$

The drone will reach the outermost engagement point in 13 minutes. Now we need to find how long it would take the fighters to reach the outer perimeter.

A normal textbook might ask you to figure out how far it is to the outer perimeter, but in this case, let's roll with the fact that the air command and the pilots would already know how far its defensive perimeters are. The outer perimeter is 250 miles away. The question is: How long would it take the fighters to travel 250 miles? Again, let's work with minutes:

$$1{,}190 \text{ miles/60min} = 250 \text{ miles/}x \text{ min}$$
$$(250 \times 60)/1{,}190 = 12.6 \text{ minutes}$$

The answer to the first part of the question, then, is they could wait only 0.4 minutes (24 seconds) before launching. To answer the second part about the inner defense perimeter, though, we need to rerun the calculation for how long it would take the jets to reach it. We can run this from the result we already obtained:

$$250 \text{ miles}/12.6 \text{ minutes} = 200 \text{ miles}/y \text{ minutes}$$

That comes out to 10.1 minutes. That means the colonel could wait $(13 + 4.1) - 10.1 = 7$ minutes until she orders the jets to launch and destroy the drone at the inner perimeter.

Explosion and the speed of sound

We see algebra coming into play in another interesting place: situations where naval or private research vessels move about at the intersection between ocean and sky. Imagine that as a Navy vessel is traveling, there is a surface explosion that registers from off in the distance to starboard (the right side of the ship if you are facing forward). The deck sensors register the sound of the blast about 24 seconds after the sounds register on the vessel's underwater sensors. In order to calculate the distance of the blast, and make decisions about how to respond, they would run a quick crunch of the relative speeds of sound through air and water.

In air, sound travels about 1,100 feet per second, and in the water, it travels about 5,000 feet per second. (Everyone who thought that was a mistake a minute ago when I said the water sound came first, raise your hand. That messes with people's heads all the time. Water is faster. Play along and look it up later.) We can define the speeds as:

$$S_w = 5,000 \text{ ft/s}$$
$$S_a = 1,100 \text{ ft/s}$$

The water equation is the easiest one to set up. We know that the sound was traveling for however many seconds at a speed of 5,000 ft/s.

Which gives us:

$$d = S_w t$$
$$d = 5{,}000 \text{ ft/sec} \times t$$

where d is distance in feet and t is time in seconds.

In the case of the air, it was traveling for the same amount of time as the water noise and an extra 24 seconds longer, but it was only going 1,100 ft/s:

$$d = 1{,}100 \times (t + 24)$$

Since they both started from the same place, we can set them equal to each other to see how far away that must have been, and then we solve to find t.

$$5{,}000t = 1{,}100 \times (t + 24)$$

Divide both sides by 1,100:

$$4.54t = t + 24$$

Subtract t from both sides:

$$3.54t = 24$$

Divide both sides by 3.54:

$$t = 6.78 \text{ seconds}$$

Now we plug that back into one of the equations to find the distance.

$$d = 5{,}000 \text{ ft/sec} \times 6.78 \text{ sec}$$
$$d = 33{,}900 \text{ ft} = 6.4 \text{ miles}$$

The fleet moves to intervene if needed, and then continues on its long, slow journey to keep some far corner of the world safe and stable.

Communications

How would we figure out the amount of work that has to go into launching a 6,000 kg satellite to an orbit height of 12,000 km?

The first step is to find the gravitational value when it is on the Earth. The normal equation for gravitational force is:

$$F_g = \frac{Gm_1 m_2}{r^2}$$

We're going to change just a couple things, making the G negative, since we're talking about the **potential** energy, and we'll change the F to E, since we're just dealing with Earth's gravity in this problem.
Giving us:

$$E_g = \frac{-Gm_1 m_2}{r^2}$$

where:

E_g = Gravitational energy on Earth, measured in **joules** (abbreviated J).
G = Universal gravitational constant ($6.67 \times 10^{-11} \text{Nm}^2/\text{kg}^2$).
m_1 = **Mass** of Earth (6.0×10^{24} kg).
m_2 = Mass of satellite (6,000 kg).
r = Radius of Earth (6.4×10^6 m).

Now we can plug in the pieces we know:

$$E_g = \frac{-(6.67 \times 10^{-11} \text{Nm}^2/\text{kg}^2) \times (6.0 \times 10^{24} \text{ kg}) \times 6{,}000 \text{ kg}}{(6.4 \times 10^6 \text{m})}$$

$$E_g = -3.75 \times 10^{11} \text{ J}$$

Next we run the same calculation, but this time we adjust the radius to include the distance above the Earth:

$$E_g = \frac{-(6.67 \times 10^{-11} \text{Nm}^2/\text{kg}^2) \times (6.0 \times 10^{24} \text{ kg}) \times 6{,}000 \text{ kg}}{(12.0 \times 10^6 \text{m})}$$

$$E_g = -2.00 \times 10^{11} \text{ J}$$

When we compare the two, we see a change of 1.75×10^{11} J.

For most of us, those kinds of numbers do not really connect in our brains. Think of it this way: this would be like picking up a small bowling ball and throwing it 7.46 miles. At average walking speed, it would take you about two and a half hours to hike over to where it landed.

Satellite speed

Of course, we can't just plop a satellite up there. To get it to circle the earth, the gravity pulling it toward the Earth has to be offset by the speed at which the satellite is trying to move forward in a straight line. At each altitude that speed will be different, so the telecommunications company needs to figure out the right speed for the altitude of 12,000 km.

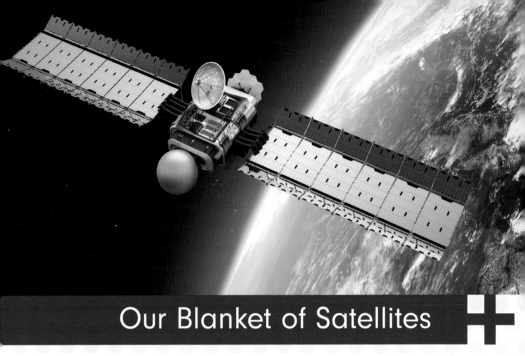

Our Blanket of Satellites

S cience fiction writer Arthur C. Clarke actually invented the idea of a satellite communications network in a paper he presented in 1954, and the Soviet Union launched the first satellite (Sputnik) in 1957.

There are currently around 1,300 working satellites in orbit around the Earth today along with approximately 2,500 non–working satellites (and a huge confetti–mess of spent boosters, old rocket and satellite parts, and so on).

These orbiting satellites are classified into three layers: Low Earth Orbit (LEO) which is between 180 and 2,000 km above the Earth, Mid Earth Orbit (MEO) located between 2,000–35,000 km, and then High Earth Orbit (HEO) with distances greater than 35,000 km. Note that even HEO is still only about one–tenth of the way to the moon (384,000 km). Satellites closer to Earth have a faster orbit because of gravity, and some satellites use thrusters to move toward or away from earth to adjust their speed for short–term missions.

The incredibly high cost of launching satellites into orbit has been an obstacle that has kept the satellite boom from growing even faster. But with recent advances in rocket technology—especially being able to re–use first stage boosters—there is likely to be an exponential burst of satellites being launched in the next few years.

The formula for this is:

$$g = v^2/r$$

where:

g = The gravitational pull on the satellite.
v = The speed the satellite is going.
r = The radius from the center of the Earth to the satellite.

We need to find how much the pull of gravity is at this distance compared to Earth's surface gravity (9.8 m/s²). 6,400 km is the radius of Earth. 18,400 km is the radius of Earth plus the satellite's orbit.

$$g/9.8 \text{ m/s}^2 = (6{,}400 \text{ km}/18{,}400)^2$$
$$g = 1.19 \text{ m/s}^2$$

Now we can plug that in to the first formula to see that:

$$1.19 \text{ m/s}^2 = v^2/18{,}400 \text{ km}$$

Multiply both sides by 18,400km to get v^2 all by itself:

$$1.19 \text{ m/s}^2 \times 18{,}400 \text{ km} = v^2$$

If we convert km to m, it will make the math easier, and then we take the square root of both sides to get:

$$v = 4{,}680 \text{ m/s}$$

That doesn't register for most of us, so let's do the conversions.

$$4{,}680 \text{ m/s} \times 1 \text{ km}/1{,}000 \text{ m} \times 0.6 \text{ mi}/1 \text{ km} \times$$
$$60 \text{ s}/1 \text{ min} \times 60 \text{ min}/1 \text{ hr}$$

When we cancel the units and crunch the numbers, we find that the satellite has to be going:

$$v = 10{,}469 \text{ mph}$$

If a car on the ground were driving that fast, it could go all the way around the equator in a little less than two and a half hours.

Comparing phone plans

The last example of the way math is mixed in with the wireless signals all around us has to do with a common challenge: choosing between three different deals on cell phone service. All of them come with unlimited text and unlimited minutes, so the decision can be based on these other criteria:

	Network Coverage	Speed	Up Front $	Monthly $
Plan A	80%	2.5G	$45	$19.99
Plan B	85%	2.5G	$25	$28.00
Plan C	95%	2.5G	$28	$25.00

Part of the trick here is that you are trying to compare some things that aren't all measured in the same way. There are two different ways you can solve that problem. One is to give different importance values to each of the variables, and a second is to translate each of these into a variable that we can measure. Let's walk through the second one to see what it would show us. (You might find it interesting to mark down the one you think will end up being better before you go on to see how we attack the problem.)

A good strategy here is going to be to translate the network speed into a percentage value, and for our purposes, we'll pretend 3G is the best available.

If all three plans come with a one-year contract, we can work from there to see what the monthly value would be for each of the plans. In a normal introductory version of the problem, you would first look to see which one would be cheaper. Doing that here would give us a frame of reference, and then we can build on that.

$$\text{Plan A} = \$45 + \$19.99/\text{month}$$
$$\text{Plan B} = \$25 + \$28/\text{month}$$
$$\text{Plan C} = \$28 + \$25/\text{month}$$

Then, to see which one is better, compare Plan A and Plan B:

$$45 + 19.99m = 25 + 28m$$

Then we solve for m. In this case, we would start by subtracting $25 from each one.

$$20 + 19.99m = 25m$$

Subtract $19.99m$ from both sides:

$$20 = 5.01m$$
$$3.99 = m$$

So, costs for Plan A and B would be even at the end of month 4. Which one would end up costing more by the end of the year?

$$\text{Plan A} = 45 + 19.99 \times 12 = \$284.88$$
$$\text{Plan B} = 25 + 28 \times 12 = \$361.00$$

Your smartphone has more processing power than all of NASA's computers in 1969—the year of the moon landing.

So, there you go. Easy, right? Well, you're probably not falling for that. In fact, we should go on to take into account the other variables. Let's see what happens if we go ahead and convert the numbers like 2G and 3G into percentages. These don't represent percentages of data or anything concrete. They're just a way for us to show the measurement of how close or far we are from our ideal plan.

Since our imaginary model has 3G as the best, we'll set that at 100%. Then the others will be 83% (from 2.5/3). We'll multiply that by the area coverage. So, for one year:

Plan A = 0.80 × 0.83, and we're getting that
for a cost of $284.88

Plan A = 0.66 from our ideal coverage–speed,
for a cost of $284.88

That means $4.36 per percentage point of value.

Plan B = 0.85 × 0.83 and we're getting that
for a cost of $361.00

Plan B = 0.7055 from our ideal coverage–speed,
for a cost of $361.00

So in this case, it comes out to $5.11 per percentage point of value. It turns out that Plan A is still a better bargain when viewed in terms of value per dollar. I think you see how it *could* have turned out the other way, and you *might've* made a bad decision by just not taking the other elements into account. If you want to duke it out between Plan A and Plan C, please do. I think you can manage that without me looking over your shoulder.

The Earth Itself

When a volcano erupts, sometimes it will throw up bombs— globs of molten lava. The scientists studying this eruption see that they can model the height the bombs are thrown by equations like the following:

$$(h)t = -9.8t^2 + 100t + 4$$

where:

t = Time in seconds.

To find the points where this crosses the x-axis, let's plug it into the quadratic formula:

$$x = \frac{-100 \pm \sqrt{100^2 - 4 \times -9.8 \times 4}}{2 \times -9.8}$$

$$x = \frac{-100 \pm \sqrt{10,156.8}}{2 \times -9.8}$$

$$x = \frac{-100 \pm 100.78095}{2 \times -9.8}$$

$$x = \frac{0.78095}{-19.6} = -0.03984$$

$$x = \frac{-200.78095}{-19.6} = 10.249393$$

Now find the midpoint of those two values, which will tell us at what time they reached their peak:

$$P_m = (x_2 - x_1)/2$$
$$P_m = (10.24393 - -0.03984)/2$$
$$P_m = 5.14 \text{ seconds}$$

When it comes to problems like, "This train left at noon going warp 3, and another train left later going fast enough to make the Kessel Run in 12 parsecs," earthquakes probably win the prize. By registering how far apart the two different kinds of **seismic** waves reach the research center, scientists calculate back to see how far away the earthquake must be. Then, they draw a circle with a radius that big. Then when other stations do the same thing, they can all look to see where their circles overlap—like a giant **Venn diagram!** This also gets a prize for the best use of circles without actually having to use π for anything.

So, let's consider one in action. An earthquake goes off, sending primary waves rippling out at close to five miles per second, and then secondary waves at about 3 miles per second. If the two waves register at the research station twelve seconds apart, how would they calculate how big to make their circle's radius?

W_p = Primary wave travel rate.
W_s = Secondary wave travel rate.
t = Time the waves have been traveling (in seconds).

We can set them equal to each other like this:

$$W_p t = W_s \times (t + 12)$$

Then we substitute in the data we have been given:

$$5 \text{ mi/s} \times t = 3 \text{ mi/s} \times (t + 12)$$

Distribute the 3:

$$5t = 3t + 36$$

Next, we'll drop $3t$ from both sides into the earthquake crevice:

$$2t = 36$$

Then divide both sides by 2:

$$t = 18$$

A quick check shows us that the math is correct. It also calculates the radius that the center will need to draw on a map:

$$5 \times 18 = 3 \times (18+12)$$
$$90 = 90$$

The radius needs to be ninety miles long.

It's kind of amazing to realize that when we pull out a cell phone or connect to the Internet, there are satellites hurtling through space at mind-blowing speeds to carry out our bidding. And when you walk down the street or drive to visit relatives, and things are peaceful, you can imagine the aircraft carriers with numbers churning in their wake as they cut through the ocean, or jet planes leaving trails of calculations trailing across the evening sky.

Math helps to keep all the backstage things, like the props and equipment, running smoothly so we can create an amazing life story.

THREE

Algebra in Others' Everyday Lives

C hapter Two was a look at some of the ways numbers help to create the flexible, interactive scenery that frames our lives. Now let's explore some of the ways that other people take up math as a tool to help them have an easier and more successful time in their careers. Of course some of this will be closely related to things we examined in the last chapter. Part of the reason our life-o-sphere exists is precisely because of the way other people have taken up math and used it to do stuff.

Airline Pilots

The career of pilots can be very different depending on whether they are military or civilian pilots, on what kind of plane they fly, and so on. For this section, we are primarily focusing on commercial airline pilots. The job usually entails inspecting the plane before flights, communicating back and forth with air traffic control, and, of course, flying the plane. It's not quite as simple as it sounds, because that last item has a bunch of smaller items that are involved, like monitoring the different dials and displays and making adjustments; managing the flight crew; and making changes to flight plans due to weather conditions, equipment malfunction, or some element of disruption among the passengers. In addition to taking off and landing the plane, which can be the hardest, most demanding skill set, the pilot (and copilot) must also take an active role in communicating a variety of information.

Take-off ground speed versus altitude

The density of air is different at different altitudes. As a result of the air pressing back against things less in higher altitudes, planes have to accelerate to a faster speed on the runway in order to become airborne. One rule of thumb to use here is that it takes about 3% more ground speed per 1,000 feet of elevation. This assumes we do not also have to adjust for differences in the wind and in the temperature, both of which can also affect how much speed is needed.

So, we can use the formula:

$$V_n = V_s + 0.03 V_s A$$

where:

V_n = Takeoff speed at some particular altitude.
V_s = Takeoff speed required if that plane were at sea level.
A = The altitude above sea level (in thousands of feet).

If we know that this plane needs to be going at a speed of 120 mph to take off from the San Francisco airport, which is at sea level, then how fast would it have to be going to take off from Denver International Airport, which is at 5,430 feet?

$$V_n = V_s + 0.03V_sA$$
$$V_n = 120 + (0.03 \times 120 \times 5.43)$$
$$V_n = 120 + 19.548$$
$$V_n = 139.548 \text{ mph}$$

A related problem comes up once the pilot is in the air, because sometimes the airspeed indicator can be affected by changes in the **atmospheric** pressure at different altitudes. Pilots can estimate their true airspeed by using the indicated airspeed on their instruments and then adding about 2% for every 1,000 feet of altitude. Notice that this is close to the takeoff problem above, but the numbers are slightly different because of the way air flowing over the wings has an additional effect. If the pilot maintains a constant reading of 200 mph on his dial as his plane is climbing to cruising altitude of 10,000 feet, what would the graph of his real airspeed look like?

If you think about what the equation would look like, it's going to be *almost* the same as the last one, just changing out the 0.03 and putting in 0.02, and changing the subscript tags:

V_a = Actual air speed.
V_d = Air speed according to the dial.
A = Altitude in thousands of feet.

$$V_a = V_d + 0.02V_dA$$

To envision what the graph looks like, we need to calculate a couple data points and then use the slope formula to find how steep the line is. We know the dial speed is 200 mph:

$$V_a = 200 + (0.02 \times 200A)$$

The plane is currently at 2,000 ft. So we'll plug in 2 for that part of the equation.

$$V_a = 200 + (0.02 \times 200 \times 2)$$
$$V_a = 200 + 8 = 208 \text{ mph}$$

Now we need to repeat that with a different altitude. Let's go with 8,000 ft.

$$V_a = 200 + (0.02 \times 200 \times 8)$$
$$V_a = 200 + 32 = 232 \text{ mph}$$

That means we now have two data points: $(2, 208)$ and $(8, 232)$.

The Development of Flight

O n December 17, 1903, Orville Wright managed his first powered flight that went 120 feet (36.6 meters) and lasted all of twelve seconds. That sounds short, but try this: imagine you are floating in the air, wobbling about a bit with unsteady balance. Maybe even hold your breath. Then count out twelve seconds in your head. Since that first flight, the development of aircraft has grown **exponentially**. Can you imagine how mind-blowing it would be for the Wrights to see aviation now?

In just over one hundred years, military aircraft have come far, indeed, from the triplane flown by the Red Baron in WWI. It was just an inch short of 19 feet (5.8 m) long with a maximum speed of 103 mph (166 kmh). Contrast that with the modern jet fighter discussed in Chapter Two, or, even more amazing, the X–15, which still holds the record for the fastest manned flight at 4,520 mph (7,274 kmh)—6.72 times the speed of sound!

On the commercial side of airline development, currently the largest airliner is the AN–225 Mriya. This plane is 275 feet long (83.8 m)(almost the length of a football field) and can reach a top speed of 528 mph (850 kmh). There is a plane in development as of .

The formula for slope is:

$$m = \frac{\text{rise}}{\text{run}} = \frac{y_2 - y_1}{x_2 - x_1}$$

So:

$$\frac{232 - 208}{8 - 2}$$

$$\frac{24}{6} = 4$$

That means the slope of the line is 4, telling us that for each increase of 1,000 feet in altitude, the true airspeed would be going up by 4 mph. How far off is the dial from accurate, then, at 10,000 feet? If you use the original equation above, you'll find it's underreporting the speed by 40 mph.

Auto Mechanic

Automotive mechanics, sometimes referred to as service technicians, are primarily focused on repair and preventive maintenance of different kinds of vehicles. Here, we are focusing on the group that would handle personal automobiles, though some of the ideas and examples would apply to people who work on big trucks, commercial fleets, or even specialized vehicles (such as construction). Some of the more common parts of a mechanic's job would include: conducting computer **diagnostics** of the car or truck; using charts, graphs, and tables in technical manuals; and running tests on different parts and systems to chase down malfunctions or to get ahead of them in some way. They change fluids, belts, and parts. They also handle different support functions

The average American spends just over $8,500 per year on automobile maintenance and upkeep.

like scheduling customer repairs, managing inventory, and ordering supplies, and learning about ongoing developments to stay up-to-date on the industry's best practices.

Manual drive train and axles

This first example is really a great introduction to the nature of a mechanic's perspective in his or her day-to-day work. In this problem, the mechanic is walking through the calculations concerning how a given number of revolutions per minute (rpm) of the engine translates to a particular mph value once the rubber meets the road.

In troubleshooting to see if there is a gap or lag in the drive train, the mechanic needs to calculate how fast the car should be traveling if the engine is running at 4,000 rpm in each of the gears. To do that, let's start with a nice, long formula:

$$S_t = \text{rpm} \times \text{engine–transmission ratio} \times \text{rear–axle ratio}$$
$$\times \text{tire circumference} \times 1 \text{ mile}/5{,}280 \text{ ft}$$

We'll pick the ratio for third gear. Given the rpm's = 4,000, the ratio for third gear is 1/1.25:

$$= 4{,}000 \text{ rpm} \times 1/1.25 \times \text{rear–axle ratio} \times \text{tire}$$
$$\text{circumference} \times 1 \text{ mile}/5{,}280 \text{ ft}$$
$$= 3{,}200 \text{ rpm for transmission} \times \text{rear–axle ratio} \times \text{tire}$$
$$\text{circumference} \times 1 \text{ mile}/5{,}280 \text{ ft}$$

The transmission/rear axle ratio is 3.73:1, so:

$$= 3{,}200 \times 1/3.73 \times \text{tire circumference} \times$$
$$1 \text{ mile}/5{,}280 \text{ ft}$$
$$= 857.91 \times \text{tire circumference} \times 1 \text{ mile}/5{,}280 \text{ ft}$$

Then we multiply that number by the circumference of the tire. These are 25-inch tires, so:

$$25\pi = 78.5 \text{ in circumference}$$

So how many times the tires rotate in a minute × distance of one revolution is:

$$857.91 \times 78.5 \text{ in} = 67,345.94 \text{ inches per minute}$$

Let's translate that to mph, since we're measuring against the car's measured speed:

$$67,345.94/12 \text{ inches/ft} = 5,612 \text{ feet}$$

Then we need to convert from feet to miles:

$$5,612/5,280 = 1.06291 \text{ miles/minute}$$

Then, convert from miles/minute to miles/hour:

$$1.06291 \text{ miles/minute} \times 60 \text{ minutes/1 mile}$$
$$= 63.77 \text{ mph}$$

This allows the mechanic to compare the "correct" speed of car and its current performance speed. Think about this question: if you decided to upgrade your ride with bigger wheels, what would be the effect? Would you move faster or slower at the same rpm's?

This is such a great example because this problem is not actually calculated by the mechanic each time. Most of the time she would just look for a table or chart in the tech manual for this make and model. However, it is important for the mechanic to understand what that table or chart represents in terms of a real

Meet Mark Cann

Let's take a break and read a few thoughts about math on the job from Mark Cann, owner of Mark Cann's Automotive.

Glad you could be with us today, Mark. Can you tell us what kind of special qualifications you have and how long you've been doing this job?

Sure, I'm an ASE Certified Master Automotive Technician. I've owned my own shop for eight years now, but I've been a mechanic for thirty-three years.

So, what does math have to do with fixing broken cars and preventing cars from becoming broken?

Quite a bit. It's not always punching in a calculator, but things like reading and interpreting a multitude of **gauges**—pounds per square inch (PSI) used in air conditioning, tires, fuel pressure, compression tests, cooling system pressure, and vacuum. There are electrical measurements like volts, amps, watts, resistance, cycles, frequency, and pulse width. Oscilloscopes display live graphing of electrical currents. Understanding these various graphs and gauges is crucial to my trade.

Conversion comes into play quite often: metric to standard, weights, fractions to decimals, and vice versa. An occasional trickier algebra problem comes up. Percentages come into play both in the shop and in the office.

Is there a kind of math problem that you find a little more like puzzle-solving and less like work?

Reading oscilloscope patterns is quite entertaining, I have to say. I love to see that line go up and down in real time. When checking a throttle position sensor with a scan tool, it is possible to make that line dance up and down the display by pushing on the gas pedal. As you push on the accelerator pedal, the readout on the graph should correspond with what you do. A test is to slowly push the pedal to the floor while watching the line move up. A bad sensor may just drop off at a certain point or the line will suddenly drop. That's fun stuff because you then know you have found the problem.

What math skill do you wish you could build up more?

As I mentioned before, slightly harder bits of algebra come up from time to time. If I don't think through that problem correctly, then the car or transmission in that differential might lock up, and there could be some very real consequences. Lives and/or lots of money are at stake.

life situation, as that aids in more accurate troubleshooting and more comprehensive prevention.

Adjusting the coolant levels

A different kind of puzzle to solve has to do with getting the right mix of coolant and antifreeze in the car. For instance, say a car comes into the shop, and the cooling system has 11 liters of coolant with 15% antifreeze. Some mechanics would just flush out the whole thing, but that can be wasteful and cost the customer more. The mechanic can plug in a few numbers to remove just part of the current coolant mix, so when she adds some pure antifreeze, it will bring the total up to 25%.

At the beginning, there are 11 liters of coolant mixture in the system, and it needs to be that at the end, too. That means it's time to sprinkle some variables out on the page:

x = The amount of 15% antifreeze to remove.
y = The amount of 100% pure antifreeze to put in.

We also need the amount of remaining mix that is staying put: $11 - x$. So now we can make an equation:

$$0.15 \times (11 - x) + 1.0y = 0.25 \times 11$$
$$1.65 - 0.15x + y = 2.75$$

Now in this case, because the amount we take out and the amount we put back is the same, we can substitute x and y.

$$1.65 - 0.15x + x = 2.75$$

Squash some like terms together:

$$0.85x = 1.1$$

Divide everything by 0.85:

$$x = 1.294$$

So, the amount of the original coolant to drain out and substitute in with pure antifreeze is 1.294 liters.

If you brake it, you buy it

This time, we'll look at two closely-related puzzles. A customer brings his car in after the third time he felt the brakes behaving badly.

The mechanic hooks up a pressure gauge to the master cylinder and compares that to a gauge hooked up to the brake cylinder on one of the wheels. The technical manual for this make and model of car says there should be a 10% (or more) drop in pressure between the front and the back. When the mechanic tests it, the front is showing 900 pounds, and the back is showing 820 pounds. He has to run a quick calculation of the percent change to see if the cylinders meet specifications. The formula for percent change is:

$$C_p = \text{(Ending value} - \text{Beginning Value)} / \text{Beginning Value}$$

If it's positive, then that means a percent increase; if it's negative, that means the result was a percent decrease. In this case, we are expecting a negative.

$$C_p = (820 - 900)/900$$
$$C_p = -80/900 = -0.0889$$

Remembering that decimals to percents works like dollar and cents, so .0889 is 8.89 percent. Since the target was 10%, it turns out that the brakes do need some work.

While they're talking, the customer mentions that he wondered if the brake pads might be wearing down and causing the trouble. He says it seems like a couple years since he brought them in to be replaced, so the mechanic pulls off a wheel to take a look.

There are 3 millimeters of brake pad left. Since they start out at 10 mm, that sounds like he's only a little more than 2/3 down and should have about another year left. Not really, though. The mechanic explains that there are really only 9 mm to work with, because there is a squeal tab that sticks up from the brake drum about 1 mm. It starts making a loud noise when the pads are down to one millimeter so drivers will know to get in for service before the braking is down to metal on metal (which is way more expensive to fix!).

First, let's see how fast we've really been going down. At 20,000 miles since the last replacement, the pads have used 7 mm. So how long will it take to use up the 2 mm before the squeal tabs start squealing? We have one ratio and we're missing part of another ratio. Hmm ... this sounds like a job for cross-multiplication!

$$7 \text{ mm}/20{,}000 \text{ miles} = 2 \text{ mm}/x$$
$$(2 \times 20{,}000)/7 \text{ mm} = 5{,}714 \text{ miles}$$

But wait, there's more! How long can the customer drive until his brakes start squealing?

$$2 \text{ yrs}/20{,}000 \text{ miles} = y \text{ years}/5{,}714 \text{ miles}$$
$$2 \text{ yrs} \times 5{,}714/20{,}000 = 0.57 \text{ years}$$

The mechanic advises the customer that he should budget for brake pads a couple weeks short of seven months to avoid the squealing and maintain optimal road safety.

Firefighters not only go through intensive classroom training but must also pass a rigorous physical test to qualify. Algebra can aid your training process.

Firefighter

Firefighters work primarily to contain and extinguish fires and to serve as first responders in an emergency. Some of the other aspects of their job include providing public education and safety training, cleaning and maintenance of vehicles and equipment, inspection and testing of equipment, and continuing to train and practice. On the scene of a fire or other emergency, the routine tasks range from connecting hoses to hydrants and climbing ladders, to working to clear and analyze fire sites.

Hose pressure

Let's start by looking at an example of the math that's actually involved when the firefighters get to the scene of a blaze. If there are 200 feet of hose going downhill from the engine with six valves, what pressure does the engine need to generate in order to maintain a nozzle pressure of 100 psi (pounds per square inch)?

The big equation is:

$$EP = DNP \pm HG \text{ (or } HL) + FL$$

where:

EP = Engine pressure.
DNP = Desired nozzle pressure.
HG / HL = Head gain / head loss.
FL = Friction loss.

Let's build the pieces needed to plug in here. The conversion estimate for the amount of pressure caused by one foot of water is: 1 ft = 0.5 psi.

Using that, they can calculate the amount of pressure added to the system by the fact that water in the hose is going downhill—this is called "head gain" versus "head loss."

$$HG = 200 \text{ ft} \times 0.5 \text{ psi}/1\text{ft}$$

The ft measurements cancel, leaving:

$$HG = 100 \text{ psi}$$

Now they have to account for the amount of loss caused by friction inside the hose. The ratio is 5 psi / 1 fitting, so Friction Loss is:

$$FL = 6 \text{ fittings} \times 5 \text{ psi}/1 \text{ fitting}$$

This time "fittings" cancels out (one on top and one on bottom), so *FL* = 30 psi.

$$EP = DNP \pm HG \text{ (or } HL) + FL$$
$$EP = 100 \text{ psi} - 100 \text{ psi} + 30 \text{ psi} = 30 \text{ psi}$$

The engine pressure has to be 30 psi. That makes sense, right? We want 100 psi. The water going downhill does that, so the engine pressure needed goes down by that much. Then we just have to compensate for the hose friction.

It might seem a little surprising that there could be so much friction inside a hose. What happens, though, is that the inside of the hose has a given amount of texture. As the water moves in and out of the tiny dips, it slows and shifts direction, causing the molecules to bump and crash into each other.

In fact, the impact of the friction varies **inversely** to the fifth power of the hose diameter. For example, if the water flow rate stayed the same, but we doubled the diameter of the hose, the friction would change by $(\frac{1}{2})^5$—so 1/32 as much friction as there was in the smaller hose. This is important because friction loss is per 100 feet of hose. A 300-foot hose of 2½-inch diameter has 15 psi FL, so the impact to the nozzle would be 3 × 15 = 45 psi.

Given what you now know about friction versus diameter, what would be the difference if a fire department switched from a 4-inch hose to a 5-inch hose with the same flow?

$$5''/4'' = 1.25$$
$$(1/1.25)^5 = 0.32768 \text{ change in friction}$$

Doing so cuts the friction loss down to less than a third of what it was. Nice!

Water rate needed

A somewhat simpler form of calculation has to be done when the fire company officer decides on the plan of attack.

$$GPM = (lw/3)i$$

where:

GPM = Gallons per minute.
l = Length of structure.
w = Width of structure.
i = Involvement, a percentage.

Consider a scenario where the team shows up to a fire at a one-story apartment building with measurements of approximately 100 feet long and 50 feet wide. The building has about 30% involvement, which is a rough measure of about how much of it is on fire. How many gallons per minute should they be using?

$$GPM = (100 \text{ ft} \times 50 \text{ ft}/3) \times i$$
$$= 5,000 \text{ ft}^2/3 \times i$$
$$= 1667i$$
$$= 1,667 \times 0.3 = 500 \text{ gpm}$$

That's the number that the team would work from when they set out their lines.

Fog nozzles

Here's a cool bit of math that is changing the way some firefighting is done when using something called a fogging nozzle. This nozzle does not actually create a fog, but instead of delivering a kind of ongoing cylinder of water, it breaks it up into smaller droplets. As a result, the surface area of water in contact with the fire and heat goes up dramatically and helps to kill the fire faster.

Let's crunch just a little bit of math to see how that would make sense.

Imagine we have a cylinder of water. Let's say it has radius of 4 inches and height of 10 inches. (Remember, it's okay to use a small model when you're illustrating an idea.)

So the surface area is going to be:

$$2\pi r^2 + \pi dh$$

That's the area of top circle and area of bottom circle, plus the area of the rectangle that bends to form the torso of the cylinder.

$$2\pi \times 4^2 + \pi \times 8 \times 10$$
$$32\pi + 80\pi = 351.86 \text{ in}^2$$

Now let's compare that to the surface area of breaking it into separate pieces. Don't worry, we're not going to dig all the way down to tiny spheres. We're just getting the feel of the effect. The math is a little long to do here, but the surface area of breaking that volume into two spheres is 384 in², which is slightly larger than the cylinder. If I break it into 10 spheres, the total surface area goes up to 659 in². Guess what happens at 100 spheres? Are you ready? 1,410 in². That's still the size of green peas, more or less. The same amount of water can cover a lot more area. Cool, right?

Special Forces

Each branch of the regular US military has special forces soldiers. There is some variation in specialties between the groups, and each of the individual soldiers on a team has a particular mix of

In modern times, with terrorism on the increase around the globe, special forces—like the SEAL team shown here—become ever more important.

skill sets depending on their specialties. To qualify as a member of the special forces, there is an extensive and incredibly rigorous qualification and training program. Once admitted to training, most members will learn some mixture of **reconnaissance**, counterterrorism, and search and rescue. On top of those things, members will take advanced training in areas like marksmanship, field medicine, demolitions, parachuting, and so on.

Marksmanship

In between mission deployments, special forces members spend time training to help keep their skills sharp.

One of those critical skills is marksmanship. Because there are so many conditions that can affect long-range precision in shooting, there is an ongoing stream of calculations going on in the shooter's head, allowing her (or him) to correct for things like wind or different target ranges.

The calculation for minutes of angle is:

$$\text{MOA change} = \text{Correction (in inches)}/\text{Distance (in hundreds of yards)}$$

So, for instance, if the target is at 400 yards, and the shot was off by 7 inches, then the adjustment would be:

$$\text{MOA} = 7/4 = 1.75$$

That means you would make the appropriate adjustment to the scope on your rifle. Keep in mind, of course, this is just one example. Real marksmen have to make similar calculations based on temperature (which makes air more/less dense, thus affecting ranges and rates of drop), humidity, wind speed and direction, and other factors. This is just to give you a feel for what kind of math is happening in the field.

Underwater dive

On an underwater approach to hostile territory, the SEAL team has enough oxygen for three hours if they are at a depth of twenty feet or less, but that drops to about five minutes if they dive down to fifty feet, because the pressure change results in the need to take in oxygen at higher concentrations. When they are about an hour into their mission, a ship is approaching, so they have to go down to a little over fifty feet to avoid being pulled into the current created by the ship's engines. If they are deep for a minute and twenty-five seconds, do they still have enough oxygen in their tanks to complete the mission? We can set up an equation:

Total capacity = Amount used prior to dive + amount used during deep dive + remaining oxygen

We'll set:

O_u = Oxygen already used up to the deep dive.
O_d = Oxygen consumed during the deep dive.
O_r = Oxygen capacity remaining.
T_{20} = Total oxygen at start of mission if at 20 feet or shallower.
T_{50} = Total oxygen at start of mission if at 50 feet (plus or minus a few feet).

So we can re-write our main equation as:

$$T = O_u T + O_d T + O_r T$$

First, let's calculate how much of their oxygen they've already consumed.

O_u/T_{20} will tell us how much was consumed prior to the incident with the boat. In this case, we know they used:

1 hour/3 hours = 1/3 of their oxygen

During the incident, they used 1 minute and 25 seconds. In this case, we have to be careful to substitute in the 50-foot capacity value, right? Which means:

O_d/T_{50} = 1 minute and 25 seconds/5 minutes

If you've ever thought your math homework was hard, trying doing it in your head while breathing through a tube in the cold, dark water!

This will be simpler if we convert to decimals:

$$x = 25 \text{ seconds}/60 \text{ seconds in 1 minute}$$
$$x = 0.4167 \text{ minutes}$$

Then we substitute that back in:

$$1.4167/5 = 0.28335$$

So let's add them together and subtract from total capacity to see how much is left:

$$3 = 1/3 \times 3 + 0.28335 \times 3 + O_r \times 3$$
$$3 = 1 + 0.85005 + 3O_r$$

We can find O_r by subtracting the values from both sides, giving us:

$$3 - 1 - 0.85005 = 3O_r$$
$$1.14995 = 3O_r$$

Divide both sides by 3, and we get:

$$0.38332 = O_r$$

The team has 38.3% of their oxygen remaining. With an hour left to go in the mission, the team still needs 1/3 of their original capacity, which would be 0.333 repeating. Since they have slightly more than that, they will be able to complete the mission.

Travel to extraction point

It's 0400 and the special forces team is moving out. As they look at the maps for the area between here and places where the helicopter can pick them up, it looks like they have 6.5 miles south down to the river, through heavy underbrush, and then they have to cut east and make their way through low overgrowth terrain along the north side of the river. They estimate about 20 percent reduced speed working their way through the underbrush to get to the river. But the second leg of the trek has a swath of light shrubs and grass, which would make for an average rate. The team is able to cover relatively level terrain with low-to-moderate overgrowth at a pace of 5 miles per hour when loaded with gear. The timeframe is tight, as the chopper will be vulnerable while it's on the ground, and the whole area will be swarming with enemy soldiers by 1030, so they have to be out before then.

What is the maximum distance east they can schedule the chopper extraction before the area is overrun by enemy soldiers moving up from the south?

We need to tackle this in two steps. If they normally make 5 mph, then their rate for the 6.5 miles down to the river would be:

$$5 \text{ miles/hour} \times 80\% = 5 \text{ miles/hour} \times 0.8 = 4 \text{ mi/hr}$$

$$6.5 \text{ miles/}(4 \text{ miles/hour}) = 1.625 \text{ hours}$$

The next leg they can travel at 5 mph, so we need to calculate back from the deadline. They have a total of six and a half hours available:

$$1.625 + x = 6.5$$

$$x = 6.5 - 1.625$$

$$x = 4.875$$

That means the team has 4.875 hours before they have to be at the extraction point. So how far is that? At 5 miles/hr × 4.875 hours, that would put them 24.375 miles east of here. Right?

No! That would put the chopper on the ground just as the enemy soldiers coming up from the south show up. Never forget that no matter how sharp the math seems, there has to be a moment where we step back and think about what is happening out in the real world. The team leader decides to set the extraction at a point 23 miles east which would buy the team a 17-minute window to get out.

Biomedical Engineer

Biomedical engineers design things like artificial organs, prosthetics to replace missing body parts, and diagnostic machines and software. In addition to designing these things, they also work to install, repair, and update/upgrade them to continually provide the best possible solutions. Some of the other key things that would fall under the role are evaluating the safety and precision of biomedical equipment, working to help researchers in medicine and biology leverage the equipment in their research, and helping train doctors and imaging technicians on proper use and care of the equipment.

MRI machines

MRI (magnetic resonance imaging) machines create images of the inside of the human body using very strong magnets and radio waves. An MRI machine with a magnet strength of 15,000 gauss (about 10,000 times stronger than the Earth's magnetic field) turns your body into a radio transmitter at 67 kHz, a little below the frequencies used for FM radio!

The contrast in the images (which tissues appear bright, and which appear dark) is controlled by setting a timing delay between when the machine transmits the radio signal into the body (think of hitting a glass with a spoon to make it ring) and when it measures the signal coming back (how loudly the glass is still ringing). The "ringing" of some tissues will die off quickly, while the "ringing" of other tissues dies out slowly.

The equation that describes this "signal decay" is:

$$S = e^{t/-T}$$

where:

e = The base of the natural logarithm, 2,71828.
S = The strength of the signal.

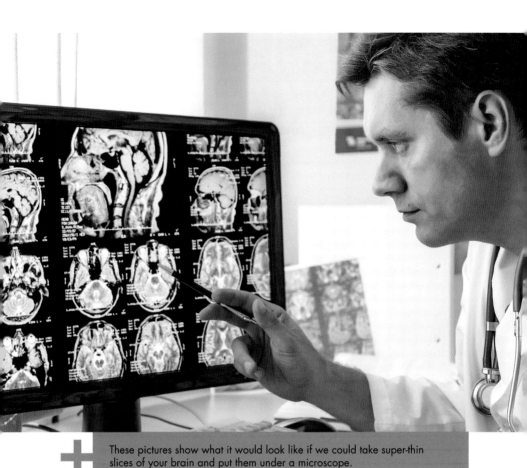

These pictures show what it would look like if we could take super-thin slices of your brain and put them under a microscope.

t = Delay time (in ms).
T = The "resonant" property of the tissue (in ms).

The negative sign tells you the signal gets weaker and weaker over time ("decay") rather than stronger and stronger.

For instance, normal liver tissue has a T of about 50 ms, whereas liver tumor tissue has a T of about 100 ms.

If you set the delay time to be too short, all tissues appear equally bright, and you can't tell one thing from another. If you

Meet Reed Busse

Reed is an MRI Applications Developer with GE
Healthcare and has been working there for ten years.

*Glad you could talk with us today, Dr. Busse. So, "engineer" sounds like
there must be a lot of math in your job. Can you tell us a little about
what kinds of math and what you need them for?*

Primarily, the math I use the most would be things like calculus,
linear algebra, even Fourier analysis. Calculus allows us to
work with the diagnostic readouts to understand where the
critical changes are happening. The linear algebra helps because
reconstructing images from MRI signals involves solving for a
large number of unknowns (the brightness of each pixel in an
image) for each different data point. Using matrices can simplify
that process a lot!

*Some of these terms the readers have probably heard, but not Fourier
analysis—what is that for?*

Think about it as if you played three notes on a piano; the sound
waves from each could be represented as a repeating cycle, but
when they're played at the same time they interfere with each
other. A Fourier transform is a way to separate those notes so we
can understand what's happening with each one.

*Is there a kind of math you wish you were better at? How would
that help?*

Linear algebra. By getting measurements at more points around
the head and body for each "ping" of the MRI scanner, you can

get higher resolution images, but it also means more equations to add to the solution. Those who understand linear algebra better are able to solve these problems and make MRI scanners faster and higher resolution.

It sounds like a cool job. What kind of special training or degrees do you need to get into biomedical engineering like you're doing?

The field needs a lot of people with college and graduate training in math, science, engineering, and computers. In my case, I have a PhD in biomedical imaging sciences. It's a great job, too, if you like helping people. I've seen improvements I've made to MRI scans used by doctors in need of new resources for their patients, and I've seen my work used as a stepping stone for further advances made by other scientists and engineers. It's also great to travel all over the world to visit universities and attend conferences.

Awesome. Thanks, Reed!

set the time for too long, all tissues appear dark, and you can't see anything. Set the time just right, and tissues will appear at different brightnesses, and you can easily tell them apart. That's called image contrast.

If you have a graphing calculator or computer, try plotting the signal from normal liver tissue (T=50ms) and liver tumor tissue (T=100ms) for a range of t from 0 to 200 ms to see where contrast (the difference of signal between normal liver and liver tumor) is greatest. You'd want to set the MRI machine to take a picture at this t to get the best diagnosis of liver cancer.

That's how you tell normal tissue from cancer, but how can you tell where the cancer is? This is done through "spatial encoding." In addition to the extremely strong magnet that's part of the MRI machine you lie inside (the one that turns your whole body into a radio-wave transmitter), there's also a "gradient coil" that makes the magnetic field stronger in one direction than the other. For instance, you can make the magnetic field a bit stronger in your head as compared to your feet, or on the right side of your body compared to your left. The strength of the magnetic field relates to the frequency of the signal. It's like the tension on a guitar string. You can control the frequency (pitch) by tightening or loosening the strings. Making the magnetic field stronger makes the frequency higher and vice versa.

The relationship between the strength of the magnetic field and frequency is known as the Larmor equation:

$$f = \gamma/B$$

where:

f = The frequency.
γ (gamma) = A constant, called the "gyromagnetic ratio," equal to 4,752 hz/gauss.

B = The strength of the magnetic field.

More important than the absolute frequency is the frequency difference (Δ, or delta) between two locations.

$$\Delta f = \gamma/\Delta B$$

You can control the magnetic field "gradient." This is represented as G. The distance between two places in your bodies can be represented by x. The difference in magnetic field strength is:

$$\Delta B = Gx$$

Therefore the frequency difference between the two locations is:

$$\Delta f = \gamma/Gx$$

The MRI machine can measure many frequencies at the same time and distinguish how much signal is at each frequency. It's as if someone hit 10 piano keys at once, some loud and some soft, and the machine listened and created a picture of which keys were played how hard. With a little bit of algebra, you can make an MRI machine do all kinds of things, and help doctors diagnose and plan treatments for a great variety of medical disorders.

Digestive solution

Here we consider the case where the patient is being given a **solution**, or a liquid in which something has been dissolved, to digest prior to testing. (And yes, these solutions do tend to taste as nasty as you would think.) Let's say we have two solutions of a chemical in water. The first is a 2% concentration, and the second one is a 10% concentration. If we are aiming for 3 liters of 3% solution, what do we do? We would define some variables, like:

x = The quantity of 2% solution.
y = The quantity of 10% solution.

And we know our overall target:

$$x + y = 3 \text{ liters}$$

Actually, we know more than that; we know the percentages of each:

$$0.02x + 0.10y = 0.03 \times 3$$

Now we solve for one of them. Let's go for x.

$$x = 3 - y$$

Then, plug that into the second equation:

$$0.02 \times (3 - y) + 0.10y = 0.03 \times 3$$
$$0.06 - 0.02y + 0.10y = 0.09$$
$$0.06 + 0.08y = 0.09$$
$$0.08y = 0.03$$
$$y = 0.375$$

So we need .375 liters of the 10% solution. That means x, the 2% solution, would equal 2.625 liters in order to add up to 3 liters total. Since we used a similar strategy to the earlier engine coolant problem, that must mean the patient is now protected against their engine coolant freezing up in the winter as well, right?

Chemicals in the bloodstream

Consider a closely related type of calculation. Let's say a tracing chemical is injected into the patient's bloodstream in order to facilitate a diagnostic scan. This chemical will stand out in pictures from the scan and make certain parts of the body easier to see. In adjusting and monitoring the settings on the diagnostic equipment, it is important to know what concentration level of tracing chemicals are present in the bloodstream. We need to find when the concentration (C) in the bloodstream will be at 0.04 mg/mL or higher at a certain time (t). In this case, the equation is:

$$C = 0.12t/(t^2 + 2)$$

So we need to set the C at 0.04 to find the time the concentration will reach the target minimum.

$$0.04 = 0.12t/(t^2 + 2)$$

Multiply both sides by denominator:

$$0.04(t^2 + 2) = 0.12t$$

Now, we'll distribute so we can split the terms.

$$0.04t^2 + 0.08 = 0.12t$$

Here we see the path home:

$$0.04t^2 - 0.12t + 0.08 = 0$$

And then we factor:

$$(0.2t - 0.4) \times (0.2t - 0.2) = 0$$

Then test both options to see what happens if we set them to 0.

$$0.2t - 0.4 = 0$$
$$0.2t = 0.4$$

Divide by 0.2:

$$t = 2$$

Now we test the other one.

$$0.2t - 0.2 = 0$$
$$0.2t = 0.2$$

Divide by 0.02:

$$t = 1$$

Testing both back in the original equation verifies, so now take a second to remember what we were after and why. I'll leave it to you to answer: What is the soonest time that the concentration would be high enough to run the scan?

Oceanographer

Oceanographers study the oceans, ice caps, and fresh water. They consider water's interconnections with the atmosphere and ecosystems. There are different specializations among most oceanographers. Geological oceanographers specialize in the sea floor. There are also chemical oceanographers and biological oceanographers. Some of the more common elements of their roles include analyzing samples of organic and inorganic material to test for pollution or toxicity; creating and studying simulations and models of various oceanic and atmospheric interactions; and, of course, teaching at universities and public forums. OK, let's see what kind of stuff these oceanographers get to use math for.

Storm waves

The height of waves can be approximated as a linear function of the length of time the wind blows over them. In a storm, there was a wind blowing at 50 mph. When the wind had been going for 8 hours, the waves were 26 ft high, and by the time the stormy wind had been going for 11 hours, the waves were up to 38 ft. How can we figure out that line and use it to predict when the waves would be expected to reach a height of 50 feet?

We know we need to start with the equation for a line:

$$y = mx + b$$

The next step, since we have been given two points, is to use the slope formula to find m:

$$m = (y_2 - y_1)/(x_2 - x_1)$$

Then we plug in the data points we've collected:

$$m = (38 - 26)/(11 - 8)$$
$$m = 12/3$$
$$m = 4$$

We can put that into the line equation with one of our points and solve to find the value of b:

Her Deepness

Dr. Sylvia Earle is an oceanographer in a class by herself. Her nickname is "Her Deepness," and she has a long, long list of awards from organizations, including being named a "Living Legend" (Library of Congress) and a "Hero for the Planet" (*Time* magazine).

She was the first prominent woman in the field and has gone on to accumulate more than seven thousand hours of dive time—both as expedition participant and as leader. She has a PhD from Duke University and more than twenty honorary degrees from places all around the globe.

There are different specializations within oceanography, and Dr. Earle's is a focus on the conservation and understanding of delicate marine ecosystems. This mission has been at the center of her work as a researcher, as the former chief scientist of the National Oceanic and Atmospheric Association, and as the director of several nonprofit organizations, not to mention founding a few of her own.

She even holds the record for the deepest untethered dive, at 1,250 feet (381 m) (which requires a special suit to keep from being crushed by the pressure!), and with her husband, she designed a submersible capable of reaching a depth of three thousand feet.

$$y = mx + b$$

$$26 = 4 \times 8 + b$$

$$26 = 32 + b$$

Subtract 32 from both sides:

$$-6 = b$$

This gives us have enough information to construct our line equation:

$$y = 4x - 6$$

To use it predict when the waves would reach a height of 50 feet, we just need to plug that value in for y and solve to find the x:

$$50 = 4x - 6$$

Add 6 to both sides:

$$56 = 4x$$

Then divide the whole crowd by 4:

$$14 = x$$

The waves would reach a height of fifty feet after fourteen hours of those strong winds—a dangerous height indeed!

Don't be fooled by Hollywood: a tsunami doesn't need to be a high, towering wave to cause lots of damage. It's often more like a wall of bulldozers.

Tsunami speed

There is also an equation that allows us to see how the speed of a tsunami is affected by the change in water depth. Let's take the following equation:

$$v = \sqrt{gD}$$

where:

g = 9.8 m/s².
D = Water depth in meters.

If we plug two different depths in, and compare the outputs, we'll be able to see the effect on the tsunami as it approaches a coastal area. So consider a point out where the depth of the ocean is 7 kilometers (7,000 meters).

$$v = \sqrt{9.8 \text{ m/s}^2 \times 7,000}$$

$$v = 261.9 \text{ m/s} = 943 \text{ km/hour} = 586 \text{ mi/hour}$$

Compare that to the much slower pace created when the ocean is 2 kilometers deep instead:

$$v = \sqrt{9.8 \text{ m/s}^2 \times 2,000}$$

$$v = 140 \text{ m/s} = 504 \text{ km/hour} = 313 \text{ mi/hour}$$

A tsunami slows down as the ocean gets shallower. That's because the waves are hitting the sea floor. Near the shore, the water then begins to "bunch up" as it's hit from behind by water that's still moving really fast, meaning the waves become much, much taller!

Diving pressure

As we go down in the water, we find the inverse of what happens to mountain climbers, where the air pressure gets thinner and thinner as they ascend. For ocean researchers and divers, the pressure goes up 14 psi for every 33 feet you go down.

$$P = d \times (14\text{psi}/33\text{ft})$$

where:

P = Pressure.
d = Depth in feet.

The average depth of the Pacific Ocean is 14,000 feet. What is the average pressure at the bottom of the Pacific?

$$P = 14{,}000 \times (14 \text{ psi}/33 \text{ ft}), \text{ giving us the value of } 5{,}939 \text{ psi}$$

At its deepest, the pressure under the ocean is equivalent to a person holding up fifty jumbo jets!

From flying through the sky faster than the speed of sound, to diving below the ocean where the pressure is as strong as being crushed by those same airplanes, and from tangled underbrush of foreign military missions to the tangled neurons inside the human brain, we see the impressive variety of places math can help people explore and understand.

CONCLUSION

W ell? What do you think? Did I convince you that algebra might actually be helpful out in the real world?

Before you head out, let's talk about you and Galileo for a minute. It is easy for us to become familiar and comfortable with things that have always been around. Algebra is, believe it or not, one of those things. Even when you didn't yet know about it, and even when you're not using it, it is there, behind the scenes, helping to make our world run. It helps pilots get their planes in air, mechanics keep our wheels on the road, and our bodies fight off disease.

More than that, though, I want you to just pause for a minute, with all these equations and applications fresh in your head. I want you to realize that at this moment you understand as much math as Galileo did in his day, and that was enough math to change the world. Let that bounce around for a minute: you know math that Plato and Aristotle didn't. Euclid didn't. Pythagoras. Take a deep breath: Leonardo Da Vinci.

You know some cool math things that Galileo would have probably been willing to give up coffee for. (OK, he probably didn't have a big coffee addiction like the rest of us, but this is my story, so remember, hobbits can have television and brilliant Renaissance scientists can have coffee!) You get the

Galileo and his friend puzzled over the mathematics of the solar system. Centuries from now, perhaps people will see you in a book like this.

idea. Something was that dear to him. So, he figures out how to create the first real telescope, and then he figures out how to fix the scientific model of the whole, big, fat, solar system. And he didn't even have all the cool stuff yet that Descartes would invent for us to use when we try to think about stuff like speed and mass. In fact, even Descartes didn't have the stuff Descartes thought up until, well, after he used algebra to think it up!

Cool fact: Galileo died the same year Newton was born, and you will probably always remember this because the square root of 16 is 4 and the square root of 4 is 2, and the year was 1642.

What happens if you keep learning about math? Algebra is the foundation for a lot of really amazing things that you can go on to learn how to do, and there are examples we couldn't fit in. We didn't learn about the math of zombie plagues or asteroids zooming toward the earth. What if you are the next Galileo helping unpuzzle part of the universe? You have to remember that a heroine starting out on her journey still learns stuff and gets better and manages to defeat bigger, more villainous villains by the end. Algebra is really the beginning of the adventure, so don't get lost in the forest, use your map, get help from the other people on your quest, and go be more awesome.

Glossary

abstract In math or logic, the removal of specific details or features to create a more generalized form.

altitude Height of an object above the ground or above sea level.

atmospheric Having to do with the atmosphere, such as the pressure caused by the layers of air covering the earth.

coefficient The number placed as a multiplier in front of some variable, as in $5x$, where 5 is the coefficient of the variable x.

conversion The process of changing from one standard of measurement to another, usually by using a proportion.

cryptography The study of creating and breaking secret codes.

diagnostic A piece of equipment or a procedure for identifying which kind of problem or illness is preventing a system from working correctly.

displacement In math and physics, this refers to the volume of water forced to move away because another object is occupying its space.

equilibrium The condition where forces acting in different directions are balanced so the net effect is to cancel each other out and the object of group of objects does not move.

exponentially Growing or increasing in a manner represented by exponents, such as $2n$.

function An equation that assigns one output value (a y) to each input value (an x)

gauge To measure an object or effect with a gauge (or to think as if doing so).

intercept To come into contact with something, usually to prevent its continuation on a previous course or direction.

interpolation Adding a new piece in between two others, like a new number on a graphed line.

inverse The opposite or the reverse of something. In math it often means the action which undoes an operation, such as multiplying by $1/x$.

joule A standard measurement of work or energy.

linear equation A polynomial expression with a leading exponent of one, such that plotting the inputs and outputs on a graph would result in a function with constant slope (a straight line).

mass Roughly, the amount of atoms of a substance in an object, measured by how hard it is to move the object.

maximum The greatest amount. In mathematical graphs it refers to the point at which the greatest y value is reached.

midpoint The point located an equal distance between two other points or values.

minimum The smallest or least amount; in mathematical graphs, it refers to the point at which the lowest y value is reached.

parabola A symmetrical curve that looks like an arch, but which can open up or down.

perimeter The outer edge or boundary of an object; also used to mean the distance or length of that boundary.

polynomial An algebraic expression with a finite number of terms and having only integers as exponents.

potential Stored up or unused capacity; amount of work or energy that is available but not yet expended.

precursor Something that came before, usually of the same or similar kind.

predictable Behaving or occurring in a way that allows future values to be guessed in advance.

proportion A relationship of equality between two ratios.

quadratic equation A polynomial in which the leading exponent is 2.

reconnaissance A preliminary survey to gather information and assess potential routes and dangers, especially regarding the size and location of enemy forces.

rhetorical The use of written or spoken words to create a desired effect.

seismic Having to do with an earthquake.

solution A mixture in which one substance is dissolved inside another.

supplemental Adding on to or completing something.

syncopated Short changes in the pattern or pace of something.

thermal Of or relating to heat, especially preventing or assisting in the transfer of heat.

trigonometry Branch of mathematics dealing with the use of triangles and circles to understand certain situations or recurring cycles of measurements.

tsunami A long sea wave caused by an underwater earthquake, landslide, or other disturbance.

velocity The speed of something in a given direction.

Venn diagram A diagram using circles to represent sets or groups. Common elements are represented by overlapping areas between the respective circles.

Further Reading

Books

Gowers, Timothy, June Barrow-Green, and Imre Leader (Editors). *The Princeton Companion to Mathematics.* New Jersey: Princeton University Press, 2008.

Jackson, Tom, ed. *Mathematics: An Illustrated History of Numbers.* New York: Shelter Harbor Press, 2012.

McKellar, Danica. *Hot X: Algebra Exposed!* New York: Penguin, 2011.

Pickover, Clifford A. *The Math Book: From Pythagoras to the 57th Dimension, 250 Milestones in the History of Mathematics.* New York: Sterling, 2009.

Simmons, George F. *Precalculus Mathematics in a Nutshell: Geometry, Algebra, Trigonometry.* Oregon: Wipf & Stock, 2003.

Websites

American Mathematical Society

www.ams.org/mathimagery/

While being a useful resource in general, the collection of examples connecting math and art is particularly interesting (and rare). Under the heading of Math Samplings, they also have a nice list of additional websites worth exploring.

Ask Dr. Math: The Math Forum @ Drexel

mathforum.org/dr.math/

This site offers a variety of basic explanations of concepts and examples. One of its strengths is that the topics are broken out by subjects and by level in school (elementary, middle, high school, college and beyond). They do a helpful job of working through sample problems and also allow you to search by topic.

Biographies of Women Mathematicians
www.agnesscott.edu/lriddle/women/chronol.htm

This site has a great collection of biographies of important women mathematicians down through history.

Get the Math
www.thirteen.org/get-the-math/

This website features videos that show how math is used in the real world. These include examples from fashion, music, and more.

Khan Academy
www.khanacademy.org

This is an excellent online learning website, and the learn-as-you-go format allows you to click on only the short instructional videos you need as you work your way through the course. There are courses at a wide range of skill levels.

Plus Magazine
plus.maths.org/content/

This online magazine is run under the Millennium Mathematics Project at Cambridge University. It offers interesting short articles on interesting problems in math (and science). The problems are complex, but they are broken down in a way that is easy to follow.

TED Ed: Lessons Worth Sharing
ed.ted.com/lessons?category=mathematics

These video talks give engaging animated presentations and explanations of various math concepts, including numbers, operations, and algebra.

Bibliography

Barnett, Raymond A, Michael R. Ziegler, and Karl E. Byleen. *College Algebra with Trigonometry*. New York: McGraw-Hill, 2001.

Bellos, Alex. *The Grapes of Math: How Life Reflects Numbers and Numbers Reflect Life*. New York: Simon and Schuster, 2014.

Berlinghoff, William P., Kerry E. Grant, and Dale Skrien. *A Mathematics Sampler: Topics for Liberal Arts*. Maryland: Ardsley House Publishers, 2001.

Byers, William. *How Mathematicians Think: Using Ambiguity, Contradiction, and Paradox to Create Mathematics*. Princeton: Princeton University Press, 2007.

Charles, Randall I. *Algebra I: Common Core*. New York: Pearson, 2010.

Clawson, Calvin C. *Mathematical Mysteries: The Beauty and Magic of Numbers*. New York: Plenum Press, 1996.

COMAP. *For All Practical Purposes: Mathematical Literacy in Today's World*. New York: W. H. Freeman and Company, 2006.

Devlin, Keith. *Mathematics: The Science of Patterns: The Search for Order in Life, Mind and the Universe*. New York: Henry Holt, 2003.

Ellenberg, Jordan. *How Not to Be Wrong: The Power of Mathematical Thinking*. New York: Penguin, 2014.

Frenkel, Edward. *Love & Math: The Heart of Hidden Reality*. New York: Basic Books, 2013.

Jackson, Tom, editor. *Mathematics: An Illustrated History of Numbers*. New York: Shelter Harbor Press, 2012.

Lehrman, Robert L. *Physics The Easy Way*. Hauppage, NY: Barron's Educational Series, Inc., 1990.

Mankiewicz, Richard. *The Story of Mathematics*. Princeton, NJ: Princeton University Press, 2000.

McLeish, John. *Number: The History of Numbers and How They Shape Our Lives*. New York: Fawcett, 1991.

Oakley, Barbara. *A Mind for Numbers: How to Excel at Math and Science (Even if You Flunked Algebra)*. New York: Tarcher, 2014

Paulos, John Allen. *Beyond Numeracy: Ruminations of a Numbers Man*. New York: Alfred A. Knopf, 1991.

Peterson, Ivars. *Islands of Truth: A Mathematical Mystery Cruise*. New York: W. H. Freeman and Company, 1990.

———. *The Mathematical Tourist: Snapshots of Modern Mathematics*. New York: W. H. Freeman and Company, 1988.

Pickover, Clifford A. *The Math Book: From Pythagoras to the 57th Dimension, 250 Milestones in the History of Mathematics*. New York: Sterling, 2009.

Rooney, Anne. *The Story of Mathematics: From Creating the Pyramids to Exploring Infinity*. London: Arcturus, 2015.

Sardar, Ziauddin, and Jerry Ravetz. *Introducing Mathematics*. Cambridge: Icon Books, 1999.

Serway, Raymond A., John W. Jewett, Jr. *Physics for Scientists and Engineers with Modern Physics, 7th ed.* Belmont, CA: Thomson Brooks/Cole, 2008

Stewart, James, Lothar Redlin, and Saleem Watson. *Elementary Functions*. Boston: Cengage Learning, 2011.

Stewart, Ian. *Nature's Numbers: The Unreal Reality of Mathematics*. New York: Basic Books, 1995.

Strogatz, Steven. *The Joy of X: A Guided Tour of Math, from One to Infinity*. Boston: Houghton-Mifflin, 2012.

Index

Page numbers in **boldface** are illustrations. Entries in **boldface** are glossary terms.

About the Author

Erik Richardson is an award-winning teacher from Milwaukee, where he has taught and tutored math up to the college level over the last ten years. He has done graduate work in math, economics, and the philosophy of math, and he uses all three in his work as a business consultant with corporations and small businesses. He is a member of the Kappa Mu Epsilon math honor society, and some of his work applying math to different kinds of problems has shown up at conferences, in magazines, and even in a few pieces of published poetry. As the director of Every Einstein (everyeinstein.org), he works actively to get math and science resources into the hands of teachers and students all over the country.